Texas

AMERICA THE BEAUTIFUL

second series

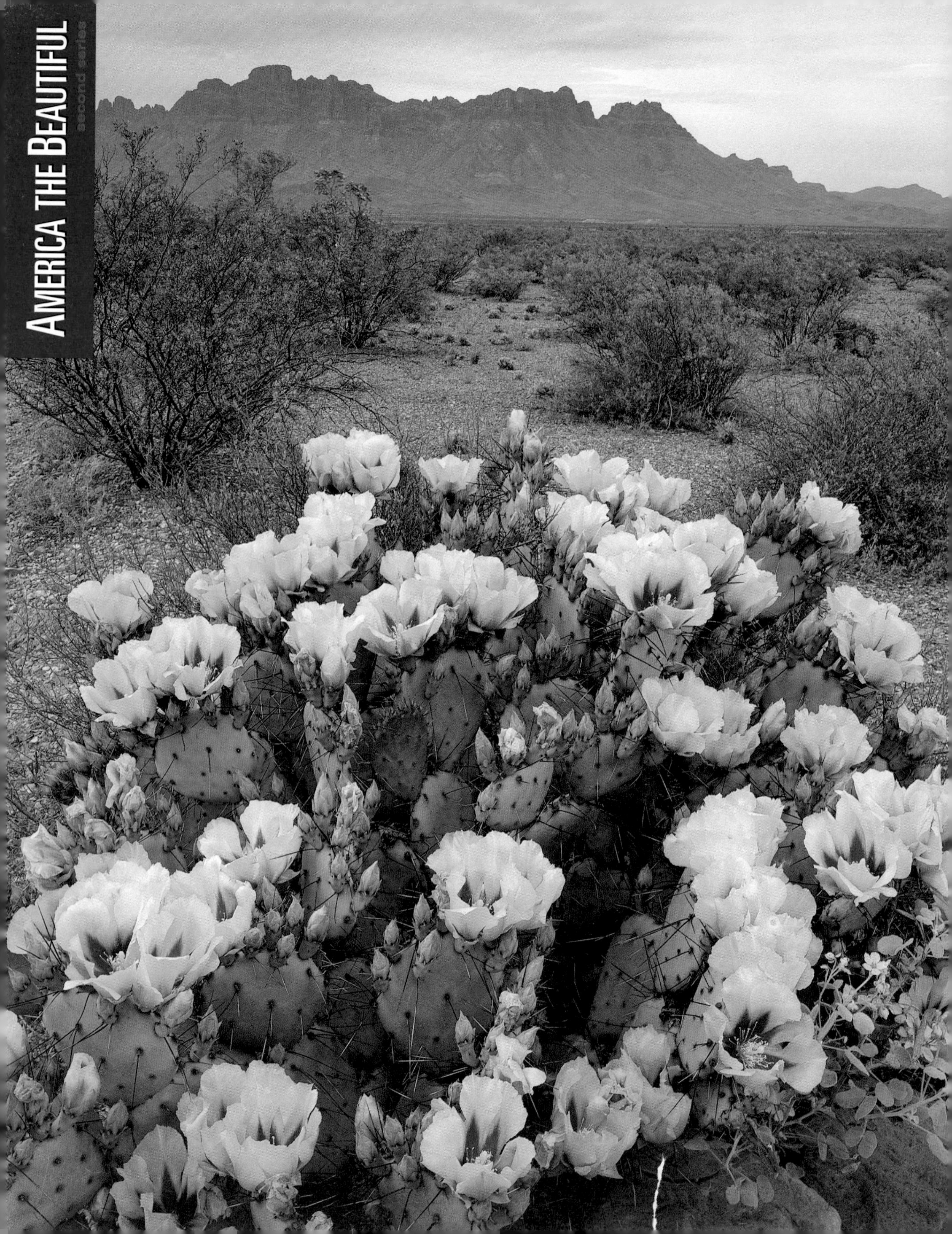

Texas

Ann Heinrichs

Children's Press®
A Division of Grolier Publishing
New York   London   Hong Kong   Sydney
Danbury, Connecticut

Frontispiece: Prickly pear cactus

Front cover: San Antonio skyline

Back cover: Bluebonnets in bloom

Consultant: Jeanette Larson, Texas State Library

Please note: All statistics are as up-to-date as possible at the time of publication.

Visit Children's Press on the Internet at http://publishing.grolier.com

Book production by Editorial Directions, Inc.

Library of Congress Cataloging-in-Publication Data

Heinrichs, Ann.
    Texas / Ann Heinrichs.
        144 p. 24 cm. — (America the beautiful. Second series)
    Includes bibliographical references and index.
    ISBN 0-516-20998-1
    1. Texas—Juvenile literature. I. Title. II. Series.
F386.3.H45 1999
976.4—dc21
                                                                98-37529
                                                                    CIP
                                                                     AC

Acknowledgments

For their kind assistance in this project, I am grateful to innumerable employees of Texas's state library and archives, department of economic development, and travel and tourism association; and to all the Texans who shared their visions and experiences with me.

Austin

Taking a ride on the beach

Big Bend National Park

Contents

Prickly pear
cactus flower

San Antonio

Cypress trees

Latinas in Texas

A mariachi

CHAPTER ONE

The Best of All Worlds

Alicia doesn't mind getting up at 5:30 every morning. The long bus ride to school gives her a chance to look over her homework and read a favorite book.

Alicia's home—in the Trans-Pecos region of western Texas—is far from the nearest school. It's also far from the big shopping centers where her family buys clothes and household supplies. Alicia keeps her own shopping list—erasers, barrettes, pet food, nail polish. She waits for the day when everyone piles into the truck for their monthly shopping spree.

Now in sixth grade, Alicia is proud of her English skills. She has been taking all her classes in English for the last four years. She even helps out with the younger students who are struggling to learn their second language.

Late in the afternoon, after another long ride, Alicia is back at home. There she speaks mostly Spanish. Her family has lived in these parts since the 1820s. One of her ancestors even died fighting for Texas's independence from Mexico.

Alicia feeds her pet armadillo, then helps her mother prepare the family's dinner. She drizzles thin layers of wheat-flour batter onto a griddle to make tortillas. Then she mixes the syrupy-sweet glaze for sopaipillas, her favorite dessert. Meanwhile, her brother climbs the rocky hills beyond their home. He herds the family's

Mexico has had great influence on Texan culture.

Opposite: The Rio Grande in West Texas

Geopolitical map of Texas

goats down from their grazing ground and locks them in their pen for the night.

Cowboys and cattle drives are common images of Texas. Cowboy hats, cowboy boots, and gaudy belt buckles are still high fashion in some parts of the state. Fights even break out over the proper cowboy recipe for "Texas Red" chili.

But none of this has much to do with Alicia—or with the millions of real Texans who make up the state today. Texans like to tell tourists that it's "like a whole other country." But the sights, sounds, smells, and tastes of Texas come from many countries. There are German sausages, Czech polka bands, Tex-Mex *tejano* music, real Mexican corn-husk tamales, and French Creole pecan pie.

How Texans earn a living has changed since the days of the Wild West too. Cowboys have been replaced by new types of adventurers. Instead of riding the open range, they work in steel-and-glass laboratories and skyscrapers. They are high-tech engineers, medical researchers, and other modern professionals.

Texas leads the United States in oil, natural gas, and aerospace industries. And no other state has as many ethnic festivals and rodeos. Texas landscapes are as diverse as its people, with deep forests, sparkling beaches, dry deserts, magnificent mountains, and endless plains. Texans like to brag that they've got the biggest, the most, and the best of everything. While they might stretch the truth just a little, there's plenty to brag about!

Texas has come to be known for its big modern cities.

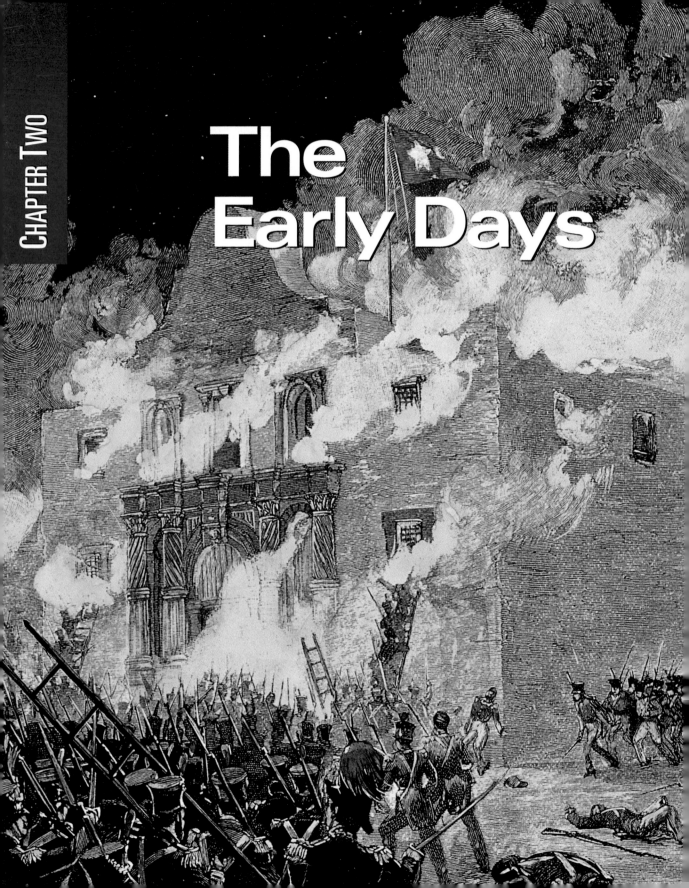

CHAPTER TWO

The Early Days

The Comanche Indians had many villages in early Texas.

hen Spanish explorers first arrived in Texas, they found several native groups. The Caddo of East Texas were the most advanced of all the Texas tribes. While other groups were nomadic— moving from place to place— the Caddo were settled in permanent farming villages. Their society was well organized, with priests, chiefs, and artisans. Various Caddo tribes formed a political alliance called the Hasinai Confederacy. It was the Caddo word for "friend" that gave Texas its name.

The Lipan Apache lived on the Edwards Plateau in Southcentral Texas. They often warred with other tribes and, later, with the settlers. Mescalero Apache ranged from Arizona and New Mexico into West Texas. The Comanche migrated into North Texas from the northern plains. They were expert horsemen, hunting buffalo and other wild animals from horseback. The Tonkawa of central Texas were hunters too.

Along the Gulf of Mexico lived the Karankawa and Attacapa. These semi-nomadic people lived mainly by fishing in the Gulf of Mexico and the streams that flowed into it. In South Texas and the lower Rio Grande valley lived the Coahuiltecan people. They built homes of adobe, or sun-dried mud-bricks. They grew corn and gathered roots, herbs, and the fruit of the prickly pear cactus.

During the 1800s, many other tribes moved into Texas as set-

Opposite: The fall of the Alamo

The Early Days **13**

Dozens of Spanish expeditions crossed the Rio Grande in search of gold. One group of explorers met up with the Caddo Indians of East Texas. The Indians called them by a name that sounded like *Tayshas*, meaning "friends." As a gesture of courtesy, the Spaniards called the Indians the same name. Spaniards spelled it "Tejas," pronounced *Tay-hahs*. Anglos later changed the spelling to "Texas." ■

tlers pushed them from their homelands. Among the newcomers were those called the Five Civilized Tribes, from the southeastern United States: the Cherokee, Choctaw, Chickasaw, Creek, and Seminole. Others were the Kickapoo and Shawnee.

Shipwrecks and Gold

Alonso Álvarez de Piñeda sailed west from Jamaica in 1519. The Spaniard's mission was to find a route to India and China. What he found instead was the Rio de las Palmas, later called the Rio Grande. Piñeda sailed into the river's mouth and mapped the Texas coast. For Spaniards, this new discovery added more territory to their colony of New Spain.

Another shipload of Spaniards was exploring the Florida coast in 1528 when a storm demolished their ship. Álvar Núñez Cabeza de Vaca, one of the few survivors, told what happened next. Hoping to reach Mexico, the handful of seamen took wood from the wrecked ship and made rafts. They used their shirts for sails and wove horses' tails into ropes to work the sails.

Cabeza de Vaca, an African named Estevánico, and two other men came ashore, half dead, on Galveston Island. Karankawa Indians surrounded them at once and made the men their slaves. But after Cabeza de Vaca removed an arrow from a

Cabeza de Vaca and his companions living with the Native Americans

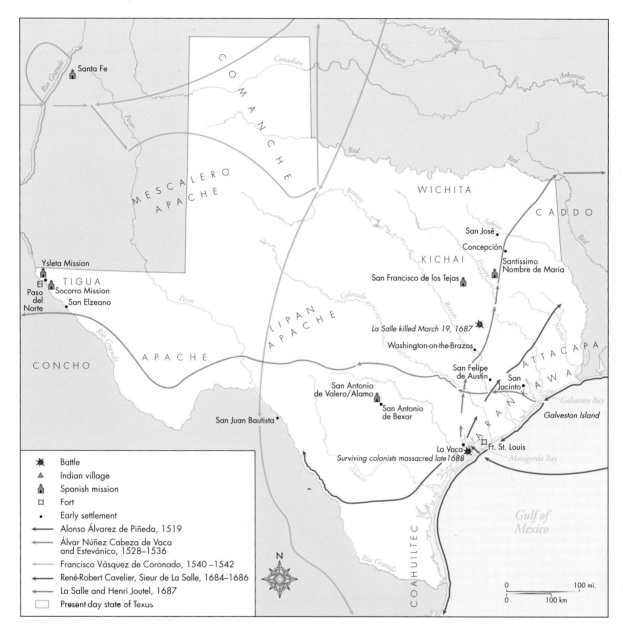

Map legend:

- ✸ Battle
- ▲ Indian village
- ⌂ Spanish mission
- ⌗ Fort
- • Early settlement
- ← Alonso Álvarez de Piñeda, 1519
- ← Álvar Núñez Cabeza de Vaca and Estevánico, 1528–1536
- ← Francisco Vásquez de Coronado, 1540–1542
- ← René-Robert Cavelier, Sieur de La Salle, 1684–1686
- ← La Salle and Henri Joutel, 1687
- ☐ Present-day state of Texas

Map labels: Santa Fe, Rio Grande, Pecos, Canadian, COMANCHE, Cimarron, Arkansas, Arkansas, Red, MESCALERO APACHE, WICHITA, CADDO, Sabine, San José, Concepción, KICHAI, Santissimo Nombre de Maria, Ysleta Mission, TIGUA, El Paso del Norte, Socorro Mission, San Elzeano, Pecos, San Francisco de los Tejas, Colorado, Brazos, Red, CONCHO, APACHE, LIPAN APACHE, Rio Grande, La Salle killed March 19, 1687, Washington-on-the-Brazos, Neches, ATTACAPA, San Antonio de Valero/Alamo, San Antonio de Bexar, San Juan Bautista, San Felipe de Austin, San Jacinto, ARAN, AWA, Galveston Bay, Galveston Island, La Vaca, Surviving colonists massacred late 1688, Ft. St. Louis, Matagorda Bay, Gulf of Mexico, COAHUILTEC, Rio Grande, N, 0 100 mi., 0 100 km

Exploration of Texas

wounded Indian, the men were seen as healers. Eventually they escaped and marched overland to what is now California. Cabeza de Vaca's book—*Naufragios. . .*, or *Shipwrecks. . .*—about the ordeal was the first published description of Texas.

Francisco Coronado's
march in 1540

Soon every Spanish explorer knew what lay north of Mexico—gold! Cabeza de Vaca told of Indian legends about the Seven Cities of Cibola, where streets were paved with gold. Indians often embellished the legend just to get the explorers to move on.

Francisco Vásquez de Coronado was fascinated by the golden tales. In 1540, he left Mexico with a fortune-hunting expedition of almost a thousand men. For two years he trekked across the Southwest, passing through northern Texas on the way. Like others before and since, Coronado returned empty-handed.

The French were exploring North America, too. René-Robert Cavelier, Sieur de La Salle, had explored the Mississippi River and was now ready to move in on New Spain. In 1685, he was shipwrecked in Matagorda Bay and established Fort St. Louis. For the next five years, France claimed the land that is now Texas. But France was unable to defend its claim, and Spain took over again in 1690.

Meanwhile, Spanish monks of the Franciscan order were on a conquest of their own. Hoping to convert the Indians to Christianity, they set up Roman Catholic missions throughout New Spain. The first mission in Texas was built at Ysleta, near present-day El Paso, in 1682. East Texas's first mission, San Francisco de los Tejas, opened near Weches in 1690. A presidio, or fort, was often

Six Flags over Texas

Six flags have flown over Texas. The Spanish flag waved over the territory from 1519 to 1685. France raised its flag for only five years—from 1685 to 1690. Then the Spanish flag reigned again from 1690 to 1821. After Mexico gained its independence from Spain in 1821, Texans lived under the Mexican flag until 1836. The Lone Star flag of the Republic of Texas waved from 1836 to 1845.

From statehood till now, Texans have lived under the United States flag—except for a four-year gap. They flew the Confederate flag (right) during the Civil War, from 1861 to 1865. ▧

built near a mission, and settlements grew up around the Spanish compound. Mission San Antonio de Valero, established in 1718, became the city of San Antonio and the Spanish capital of the province of Texas.

The First Settlement

After the United States purchased the Louisiana Territory from France in 1803, settlers wanted to move into Texas. In 1820, the Spanish governor in Mexico gave Moses Austin permission to bring in 300 families. Moses died before he could carry out his plans, but his son, Stephen, carried on. In 1822, the colonists made their first settlement, called Austin's Colony, in southeast Texas.

One year earlier, Mexico had won its independence from Spain. Texas then became a state within the new republic of Mexico. New settlers kept moving in, but their relations with Mexico were tense. In 1830, certain that the settlers had big plans for Texas, Mexico closed the territory to any new settlers. The conflicts soon led to bloodshed. In 1832, the Mexican commander at Velasco tried to stop Texans from bringing a cannon into the area. A few days of battle left several dead on both sides.

Stephen Austin

General Santa Anna ruled Mexico as a dictator and fought Texans at the Alamo.

Texans were growing more and more disgusted with the Mexican government. Delegates met in San Felipe in 1832, with Stephen Austin presiding. They drew up a list of resolutions calling for free immigration and separate statehood for Texas. Mexico rejected their requests. A second convention met in 1833 and drew up a proposed constitution. Austin met with Mexican officials to discuss the matter, but they threw him in jail.

The Texas Revolution

By the time he was released from prison in 1835, Austin was ready for revolution. General Antonio López de Santa Anna had taken over Mexico's government and now ruled as a dictator. Already, he was sending more of his troops into Texas. Texans hastily organized a temporary government and put together an army, with Austin as commander in chief.

Sam Houston, a veteran soldier from Tennessee, was drawn to the struggle. He sent out flyers around the country calling volunteers to Texas. "Come with a good rifle, and come soon," they read. "Liberty or death!"

In Texas, farmers with no fighting experience took up their rifles, too. Many of them were Mexican people who had lived in Texas for years.

The Texans took San Antonio, and the Mexican army retreated. As Santa Anna sent in more troops, about

189 rebels holed up in the Alamo, the city's old mission. For thirteen days—from February 23 to March 6, 1836—they defended the fort against a Mexican army of thousands. Among the defenders were the famous frontiersmen Davy Crockett and Jim Bowie. When it was over, not one freedom fighter was left alive.

On March 2, while the siege of the Alamo still raged, Texas leaders met at Washington-on-the-Brazos and issued a declaration of independence. They appointed David Burnet president of the Republic of Texas and Sam Houston as military commander. Blood continued to flow. In Goliad on March 27, Santa Anna ordered the execution of almost 400 Texans who had surrendered. The Goliad Massacre only spurred the rebels on. "Remember the Alamo" and "Remember Goliad" were the vengeful battle cries.

On April 21, 1836, Sam Houston led a surprise attack on Santa Anna's army at San Jacinto, and Texans tasted victory at last. Santa Anna surrendered, and Texas won its freedom as an independent republic.

The Alamo

The Alamo began as San Antonio de Valero in 1718. For thirteen long days in 1836, 189 people defended the fort against a Mexican force of several thousand. Legendary frontiersmen Davy Crockett and Jim Bowie were among those who died. Within the site is the white limestone chapel, scene of the thirteen-day battle, as well as a museum and barracks. ■

Sam Houston

Samuel Houston (1793–1863) had little education but studied law on his own. He was governor of Tennessee and lived among the Cherokee Indians for many years. Texas's struggle for independence struck his fancy. After leading the Texan army to victory in the Battle of San Jacinto, he became the first president of the Republic of Texas (1836–1838, 1841–1844). When Texas became a state, Houston served as its first U.S. senator (1846–1859). Next he was elected governor of Texas. However, he was deposed in 1861 for refusing to support the Confederate States of America. The Sam Houston Memorial Museum is in Huntsville. ■

Historical map of Texas

The Republic of Texas

The Republic of Texas lasted from 1836 to 1845. It operated as an independent nation, exchanging diplomats with several European countries. Voters elected Sam Houston as the republic's first president and Stephen Austin as secretary of state.

Things were not easy for the struggling republic. Ravaged by war, Texas needed money, but no foreign countries would extend loans. Indian attacks and cattle thieves threatened farmers on the frontier. Mexican army raids were a constant problem, as Mexico kept trying to regain its lost territory. The Texas Rangers, a band of armed enforcers, did their best to protect the growing republic. In spite of the dangers, thousands of new settlers were pouring in. Between 1836 and 1845, Texas's population grew from about 30,000 to more than 100,000.

Texas Rangers

In 1823, Stephen Austin pulled together a group of ten men to protect his settlement. They were organized as the Texas Rangers in 1835. One famous Ranger was Frank Homer, who hunted down the notorious outlaws Bonnie and Clyde. The Texas Rangers have been part of the state's Department of Public Safety since 1935. Today, more than a hundred Rangers are on patrol. They investigate serious crimes and help protect the governor. ◾

Statehood

Back in 1836, Texans had voted to join the United States. The U.S. Congress argued about Texas annexation for years, but the measure never won a passing vote. Finally, Congress made Texas an offer. It could join the Union if it came in as a state, not as a territory, and if it paid its own debts. All its public lands would belong to Texas instead of the United States.

Texans agreed to the terms on July 4, 1845, and voters ratified their state constitution on October 13. On December 29, 1845, Congress voted its final approval, and Texas joined the Union as the twenty-eighth state.

Good-Bye to the Republic

Texas became a state in 1845, but the Republic of Texas did not officially end until the next year. On February 16, 1846, the new state legislature met for the first time in Austin. In a somber ceremony, the Lone Star Flag of the Republic of Texas was slowly lowered. In its place, the U.S. flag was raised. One official at the ceremony was J. Pinckney Henderson, the first state governor. Another was Anson Jones, the last president of the republic. As he watched the new flag ascend the pole, Jones solemnly declared, "The Republic of Texas is no more." ◾

CHAPTER THREE

Spreading across the Frontier

For Mexico, Texas's statehood was a declaration of war. According to the United States, Texas's southern border was the Rio Grande. Mexico insisted that the border was much farther north, at the Nueces River. In 1846, just one year after statehood, this dispute exploded into the Mexican-American War. It ended with a U.S. victory.

The Texas Confederates fighting Union troops at Galveston in 1863

In the Treaty of Guadalupe Hidalgo, Mexico not only agreed on the Rio Grande as Texas's border. It also ceded a vast amount of land to the United States. For $15 million, Mexico gave up not only Texas, but also most of present-day New Mexico, Arizona, California, Colorado, Utah, and Nevada. Texas claimed a large chunk of this new territory. In the Compromise of 1850, the U.S. government bought the land from Texas for $10 million. This at least helped Texas to pay its debts.

The American Civil War

When the American Civil War began in 1861, eleven Southern states seceded, or withdrew from the Union, to form the Confederate States of America. Texans organized a secession convention and voted to secede, too. But Governor Sam Houston preferred a more moderate path. When he refused to swear allegiance to the Confed-

Opposite: Driving cattle in the Texas frontier

eracy, the convention dismissed him from office. Lieutenant Governor Edward Clark was sworn in as the new governor of Texas.

Texas supplied the Confederate army with tons of beef, crops, and other supplies, but not all Texans were in favor of the Confederate cause. About 2,000 Texans signed up for the Union army.

Texas Confederates waged some fierce battles during the war. Fighting on land and sea, they drove Union troops out of the seaport of Galveston on New Year's Day, 1863. In September, at the Battle of Sabine Pass, a small garrison of Confederates held back a Union force of about 4,000. The war ended with a Confederate surrender in April 1865, but the news did not reach Texas right away. On May 12–13, Texas fought the last battle of the Civil War on Palmito Hill.

Reconstruction

After the war, Texas and the other Confederate states were put under military rule. Across the South, Reconstruction programs began to rebuild the war-torn states without slavery. Texas slaves received news of their freedom on June 19, 1865, and the Freedmen's Bureau helped them resettle.

"Radical" Republican politicians, or pro-Northerners, ran the state government during Reconstruction. In 1870, Texas was re-admitted to the Union. However, old-time Texas Democrats were back in power in 1874, and many of the Reconstruction reforms were dismantled in the following years.

Indian attacks still discouraged settlers from moving into the western plains. Federal troops came in and, by 1875, subdued the last of the Indians. Now the frontier filled up fast. Once barbed wire was introduced in 1876, the ranges were not so wide-open any more.

Cowboys, Cattle Drives, and Railroads

Horses and longhorn cattle arrived with the Spanish explorers. Some animals escaped and ran wild. In time, they grew into great herds that spread across the western plains. They belonged to anyone who could catch them.

The cattle trade was important to Texas after the Civil War.

For Anglos, Mexicans, and blacks alike, life as a cowboy offered freedom and adventure. Cowboys chased, roped, and branded cattle and fended off rustlers and predators. They also rounded up wild horses, or mustangs, and trained them for riding.

Ranchers found themselves penniless after the Civil War. Yet they had plenty of longhorn cattle on hand. Soon the ranchers realized that they couldn't make a living unless they sent their cattle off and sold them in faraway markets. Thus began the era of the great Texas cattle drives. Cowboys rounded up steers and drove them north along cattle trails to railroad centers in the Midwest.

The Chisholm Trail was the main route. It ran through San Antonio, Austin, and Fort Worth, crossed Oklahoma, and ended in Abilene, Kansas. The biggest year for the Chisholm Trail was 1871, when 600,000 cattle thundered over the trail. Later cattle drives headed for Wichita and Dodge City, Kansas.

By the 1880s, Texas's new railroads put an end to the days of the cattle drives. Now ranchers could ship their cattle from depots close to home. Pioneer settlement followed the railroad lines, too, and farming spread out across the western frontier.

The Rough Riders

A handful of Texans were soon to become famous in the Spanish-American War. In 1898, the island of Cuba, off the tip of Florida, fought Spain for its independence. Theodore Roosevelt was assistant secretary of the U.S. Navy at the time, but he craved more action. He resigned his post and headed down to San Antonio. There he was authorized to raise "a regiment of cowboys as

mounted riflemen." His cavalry volunteers were known as the Rough Riders.

Not all of the Rough Riders were cowboys. They were businessmen, college athletes, miners, and lawmen—all looking for adventure. Roosevelt and his Rough Riders went down in history after their valiant charge up Kettle Hill. The battle had little effect on the war, but newspapers made the Rough Riders seem bigger than life with colorful, blow-by-blow accounts of their exploits.

Colonel Theodore Roosevelt and the Rough Riders after their charge up Kettle Hill

CHAPTER FOUR

Building the Modern State

When the Spindletop oil well let loose near Beaumont in 1901, crude oil spewed into the air for nine days straight. Even before the gusher was capped, investors were dreaming of the fortunes they could make from Texas oil. Several hundred oil companies sprang up within a year. As they drilled new wells, dozens of makeshift shantytowns grew up to house the oil-field workers.

The oil industry—as well as a growing natural gas industry—transformed Texas. New refining and manufacturing plants brought in thousands of workers. Across the state, farmers put down their plows and moved into the cities for jobs. Texas expanded its roads and railroads and dug deep ports for shipping out oil products.

Irrigation opened up farming in places where no one had thought anything would grow. In the 1920s, after just a few years of irrigation, the Panhandle was producing over a million bales of cotton a year. That helped Texas become the leading cotton-producing state in the country.

In the 1930s, along with the rest of the country, Texans suffered from droughts and the Great Depression. The state helped out by providing jobs and by giving aid to the sick, the aged, and the unemployed.

The Spindletop oil well

Opposite: Working on a gas well in South Texas

Admiral Chester
A. Nimitz

War and Rebirth

During World War II (1939– 1945), more than 1 million troops trained in Texas's fifteen military posts. The economy bounced back, too. Wartime brought a high demand for the state's petroleum and factory goods.

Texans filled some of the top spots in the Allied war effort. General Dwight D. Eisenhower, born in Denison, commanded all the Allied forces in Europe. Admiral Chester A. Nimitz of Fredericksburg commanded the U.S. Navy's Pacific fleet, and Colonel Oveta Culp Hobby of Houston organized the Women's Army Corps (WACs). She later became the first U.S. secretary of health, education, and welfare. Lieutenant Audie Murphy, born near Kingston, fought in North Africa, Italy, France, and Germany. He earned the most medals of any U.S. soldier in World War II, and later starred in films.

By the end of the war, Texas had become an industrial giant. Oil production soared, and oil-refining and chemical plants expanded. Factories turned out record numbers of ships and aircraft. With its high-tech aircraft industry, Texas was a top prospect for the nation's aerospace industry in the 1960s.

The modern electronics industry was born in Texas in 1958. At Texas Instruments in Dallas, engineers developed the silicon chip. This tiny component is the "magic" ingredient in computers, calcu-

"Ma" Ferguson

Miriam "Ma" Ferguson (1875–1961) was the state's first female governor. Her husband, James, had also been governor, but he was impeached. Ma Ferguson served two terms as the state's chief executive—from 1925 to 1927 and from 1933 to 1935. She set up relief programs for the poor and for unemployed victims of the Great Depression, and worked to conserve Texas farmland. She also fought to rid the state of the Ku Klux Klan organization. ■

lators, and millions of other electronic devices. Electronics became a brand-new boom industry in the state. Now the Austin area is called Silicon Hills because it's packed with over 1,700 high-technology electronics firms. In 1996, Korea's Samsung Electronics chose Austin as the location for its first U.S. manufacturing plant.

Tragedy and Triumph

On November 22, 1963, President John F. Kennedy paid a visit to Dallas. Citizens lined the streets to cheer as the president's motorcade passed. But their festive mood changed to hysteria as they watched an assassin's bullets rip through Kennedy's body. Governor John Connally, riding in the same car, was wounded in the attack. Years later, people still ask each other, "Where were *you* when Kennedy was shot?"

Kennedy died within hours, and Vice President Lyndon Johnson, a native Texan, was sworn in as president. Johnson attacked poverty and racism with his Great Society programs. But the most troublesome issue during his presidency was the country's involvement in the Vietnam War.

In 1964, NASA's Manned Spacecraft Center opened in Houston. Soon Americans would have another chance to say, "Where were you when . . . ?" In 1969, TV viewers around the world watched as astronaut Neil Armstrong made the first human footprints on the barren moonscape. His now-famous comment crackled across a quarter of a million miles of space: "That's one small step for man—one giant leap for mankind."

Changing Politics

For over a century, Texas had been a state of die-hard Democrats. But the aerospace and electronics industries brought new people into the state with diverse points of view. In 1978, Texans elected William Clements as their first Republican governor since Reconstruction.

Texans began to support Republican presidential candidates, too. Their electoral votes helped sweep George Bush of Houston into the White House. Bush served as vice president from 1981 to 1989 and as president from 1989 to 1993.

Modern Issues and Concerns

When oil and gas prices dropped in the 1980s, Texas's economy took a nosedive. The state raised taxes, cut spending, and encouraged other industries to fill the gap.

A problem facing Texas is the *colonias*—poor shantytowns along the Mexican border. Many of Texas's poorest citizens live there without running water or sewage systems.

Much of the nation's war on drugs takes place along the Rio

Opposite: President and Mrs. John F. Kennedy riding through Dallas just minutes before the president's assassination in 1963

Fire engulfed the Branch Davidian compound in Waco when federal agents took control of it.

Grande. In 1989, the federal government began sending U.S. Marines to the Texas border to help stop drug smugglers. This scheme was canceled in 1997 after the tragic shooting of an innocent young man who was tending his family's goats. Patrolling the border continues to be an overwhelming task for the state's law-enforcement agencies.

Texas was thrust into the national spotlight in 1993, when federal agents clashed with a religious sect called the Branch Davidians near Waco. The situation ended when the sect's compound went up in flames, leaving seventy-five dead.

Texas managed to bounce back from its oil crisis, and it learned a good lesson in the process. The state now has other industries to rely on besides oil. Electronics, chemicals, medical research, and tourism are important sectors of the economy today.

Texas is struggling to stretch its state budget to meet residents' needs. Schools are a major concern. So are social programs and job opportunities for Latinos and African-Americans. But history shows that Texans never met a challenge they couldn't face, and their courage and can-do attitude will serve them well in the twenty-first century, too.

CHAPTER FIVE

The Big Land

Texas is *big*. The states of Illinois, Indiana, Ohio, Pennsylvania, New York, New Jersey, and West Virginia could all fit inside Texas at once, with room left over. Spain, France, and Germany separately are all smaller than Texas. Texas is the nation's second-largest state. Only Alaska covers more territory. Before Alaska joined the Union in 1959, Texans could brag that their state was the biggest in the country.

The Coastal Plain

Some of North America's major land regions come together in Texas. One is the coastal plain that runs all the way down the U.S. East Coast and along the Gulf of Mexico. In Texas, the coastal plain covers the eastern two-fifths of the state.

Northeast Texas is the Piney Woods region. Much of its pine and hardwood forests belong to lumber companies and paper mills. All of Texas's four national forests are in the Piney Woods, too. Thick, spooky swamps surround the forests' many lakes and streams.

Many Texans enjoy the beauty of the state's beaches.

Opposite: An agave stands in the Texas landscape.

Putting Texas in Its Place

Texas is one of the southwestern states, along with Arizona, New Mexico, and Oklahoma. Oklahoma is north of Texas, with the Red River forming most of the border, and New Mexico lies to the west. The chunk of Texas that juts up to the north, between Oklahoma and New Mexico, is called the Panhandle. On the south, along the Rio Grande (Big River), Texas shares a 1,240-mile (1,996-km) border with Mexico. On the southeast, Texas has a 367-mile (591-km) coastline on the Gulf of Mexico. To the east are Arkansas and Louisiana. The Sabine River forms most of the Texas-Louisiana border. ■

Low marshes and coastal prairies line the Gulf coast. Houston, Texas's largest city, is about 50 miles (80 km) inland. The city of Galveston spreads out across Galveston Island.

Many long, narrow islands lie just offshore. Because they protect the coast from heavy waves, they're called barrier islands. Padre Island is the longest barrier island in the United States. With its north end at Corpus Christi, it runs for more than 100 miles (161 km) down the coast.

In the far south is the fertile Rio Grande valley. Farmers there grow fruit and vegetables all year round. Grapefruit is one of the region's most valuable crops. Brownsville, the state's southernmost city, is on the Rio Grande near its mouth.

The Central Plains

West of the Piney Woods are the low plains of north-central Texas. They're a continuation of the lowlands that stretch from the Midwest down through Oklahoma into Texas. Land in the central plains gradually rises into rolling hills. In the west, the plains end abruptly at the high, rugged Caprock Escarpment.

The Blackland Prairie runs in a strip from north to south, just beyond the coastal plain. Millions of acres of grassland once covered this prairie, which is now the richest farmland in the state. Cities that grew up in the Blackland Prairie include Fort Worth, Dallas, Waco, Austin (the state capital), and San Antonio.

The Hill Country and the High Plains

Austin and San Antonio sit at the foot of the Balcones Escarpment. This hilly ridge perches like a high balcony over the coastal low-

Texas's Geographical Features

Total area; rank	267,277 sq. mi. (692,247 sq km); 2nd
Land area; rank	261,914 sq. mi. (678,357 sq km); 2nd
Water area; rank	5,363 sq. mi. (13,890 sq km); 2nd
Inland water; rank	4,959 sq. mi. (12,844 sq km); 2nd
Coastal water; rank	404 sq. mi. (1,046 sq km); 14th
Geographic center	McCulloch, 15 miles (39 km) northeast of Brady
Highest point	Guadalupe Peak, 8,751 feet (2,667 m)
Lowest point	Sea level along the Gulf of Mexico
Largest city	Houston
Longest river	Rio Grande, 1,240 miles (1,996 km)
Population; rank	17,059,805 (1990 census); 3rd
Record high temperature	120°F (49°C) at Seymour on August 12, 1936
Record low temperature	–23°F (–31°C) at Julia on February 12, 1899, and at Seminole on February 8, 1933
Average July temperature	83°F (28°C)
Average January temperature	46°F (8°C)
Average annual precipitation	27 inches (67 cm)

lands below. On top is the Edwards Plateau. Also called the Hill Country, the Edwards Plateau is rugged land, with limestone cliffs, granite outcroppings, river valleys, and springs. Both resorts and ranches are nestled in these hills. More sheep and goats graze in the Hill Country than anywhere else in the United States.

The Edwards Plateau marks the southern end of America's Great Plains. In Texas, this region is called the High Plains. It covers the western Panhandle, continuing west into New Mexico and south into the Hill Country.

The High Plains are a high, grass-covered plateau with no trees. They were once thought to be good only for grazing cattle. But now, with irrigation from underground water supplies, farmers there grow cotton, sorghum, wheat, and corn. Amarillo and

The Texas Panhandle near Amarillo

Lubbock are the major cities. The rich oil and gas reserves of the Permian Basin lie beneath the plains of west-central Texas. Midland and Odessa are the region's business centers.

Land in the Panhandle is dry and flat. It's also called the *Llano Estacado* (Staked Plain). According to legend, when Francisco de Coronado crossed the Panhandle, dust storms were so fierce that he could hardly see where he was going. His men had to drive stakes into the ground as they went along so that they could find their way back.

The Trans-Pecos Region

Far-western Texas is also called the Trans-Pecos, meaning "across the Pecos River." El Paso, at the western tip, is the only city of any size. It sits on the Mexican border, just across the Rio Grande from Ciudad Juárez.

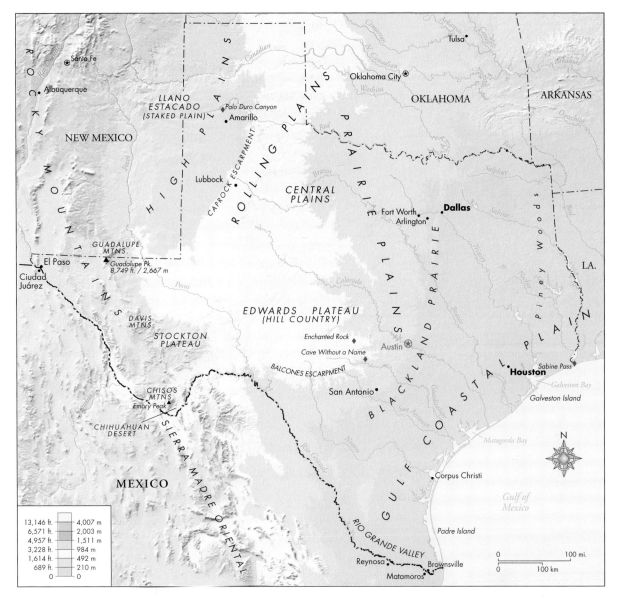

Texas's topography

High mountain ranges cut across the Trans-Pecos. They extend south from the great Rocky Mountains of western North America. These ranges continue south into Mexico, where they're called the Sierra Madre. Six mountains in West Texas rise more than 8,000 feet (2,438 m), and 100 of them are more than 1 mile (1.6 km) high.

Guadalupe Peak, the state's highest point, is part of the Guadalupe Range. Other ranges are the Davis and Chisos Mountains.

Beyond the mountains, much of West Texas is arid desert with little rainfall. But cattle graze in the level valleys, and farmers raise crops near the Rio Grande. Breathtaking canyons and river gorges cut through the wooded mountains. Big Bend National Park, in a "big bend" of the Rio Grande, preserves thousands of acres of rugged wilderness.

Guadalupe Mountains National Park

Horny Toads and Other Reptiles

The horny toad is Texas's best-known reptile. Properly named the horned lizard, it's covered with pointy spines that discourage preda-

The horned lizard is native to Texas.

tors. Horned lizards have another way to fend off enemies—they shoot blood from their eyes. But they're not as ferocious as they look—they eat only insects, and they rarely bite. If you hold a horned toad in the palm of your hand and gently stroke the stripe down its back, it flattens out and goes into a trance.

In the past, horned lizards became so popular as pets and even souvenir-shop items

Big Bend National Park

Native Americans say that, after the Great Spirit created Earth, Big Bend is where he dumped all the leftover rocks. The Chisos Mountains of Big Bend grew up as volcanoes erupted more than 50 million years ago. Emory Peak is their highest point. Pine and oak forests cover the mountains, and hikers and campers enjoy the cool air, rugged scenery, and wildlife— mountain lions, bobcats, deer, and foxes. The mountains loom above the Chihuahuan Desert, which covers much of the 801,163-acre (324,223 ha) park. Walking trails offer a glimpse of desert critters such as roadrunners, rattlesnakes, and tarantulas. Down south, in the lush Rio Grande valley, more than 430 species of birds flit through the greenery. In some spots, the river rushes through rapids and between high canyon walls. ■

that they became scarce. Now it's against state law to take a horned lizard from the wild.

More than 100 species of snakes live in Texas. The 15 types of rattlesnake, copperhead, coral snake, and cottonmouth (water moccasin) are all poisonous. The Mojave rattlesnake of West Texas has the most deadly venom of any snake in North America. Alligators are common reptiles in the state's eastern swamps.

Mammals

Sixty million buffalo once grazed the Texas plains. Now only a few small, protected herds remain. Texas bighorn sheep and pronghorn antelopes, also once plentiful, survive mainly in game preserves today. Mountain lions still roam the western mountains and the Edwards Plateau. Smaller cats—ocelots and jaguarundis—slink along the Rio Grande.

Foxes, opossums, raccoons, beavers, and white-tailed deer are common in wooded areas. Overhead, flying squirrels glide from one branch to another. They coast on the flap of skin between their

Ocelots live along the Rio Grande.

front and back legs. Other forest creatures are coyotes and javelinas—hairy pigs with tusks. On the plains, colonies of prairie dogs build "towns" with a network of tunnels that may stretch for miles.

Armadillos waddle over the hills in their armorlike shells. These relatives of the anteater dig holes in the ground to hunt for bugs. They sometimes annoy humans when they dig into lawns looking for grub worms. The best way to deal with a misplaced armadillo is to put it back in its natural habitat. Armadillos can't see or hear very well, so highway traffic kills thousands of them every year.

Near Dilley in south Texas is a "ranch" for about 700 macaques, or Japanese snow monkeys. They would have been killed in Japan, where they destroy crops. Instead, in 1972, they were transplanted to what is now the Texas Snow Monkey Sanctuary. The late author and animal activist Cleveland Amory accomplished a lifelong dream when he opened Black Beauty Ranch, west of Tyler. This refuge adopts abused and distressed animals and gives them medical care and a safe home. The animals range from elephants and bison to bobcats and coyotes. Typical residents are Nim, a chimpanzee who speaks in sign language and was rescued from a laboratory; Shiloh, a horse that once had to dive off a tower as entertainment; and Friendly, a burro who was saved from slaughter at the Grand Canyon.

Creatures of Water and Sky

Swimming in the gulf can be hazardous. Both the jellyfish and the Portuguese man-of-war inflict painful stings—even when they're dead! Hammerhead sharks lurk farther out in the gulf. But the same waters also yield tons of shrimp, crabs, clams, and oysters. Fishers take to the gulf for marlin, sailfish, speckled sea trout, and red drum. Freshwater fish include largemouth bass and crappie. The blue catfish, a favorite for fish fries, can weigh up to 40 pounds (18 kg).

Texas is the most popular state in the country for birdwatchers. Three-fourths of all American bird species either live in Texas or visit on their way through. Birds from all over the Western Hemisphere stop in Texas while they're migrating. The area around Galveston Bay is a favorite spot for hundreds of traveling species.

Long-legged roadrunners would rather run than fly. People see them speeding along the roadways at up to 15 miles (24 km) an hour. Endangered golden eagles, bald eagles, and peregrine falcons soar high over the plains. Some of Texas's tiny hummingbirds migrate from Mexico across the gulf. Pileated woodpeckers hammer away at the trees in the Piney Woods. Local folks call them peckerwoods. And the Chisos Mountains are the only U.S. nesting site for the rare Colima warbler.

Twenty million bats live in Bracken Cave in San Antonio. But the world's largest colony of city bats lives under the Congress Avenue Bridge in Austin. As many as 1.5 million Mexican free-

Roadrunners can travel as fast as 15 miles (24 km) an hour.

The Whooping Crane Refuge

Aransas National Wildlife Refuge is a winter home for the rare whooping crane. This 5-foot (1.5-m) crane is the tallest bird in Texas. It spreads its wings 7.5 feet (2.3 m). ■

tailed bats make their homes there. The citizens don't mind them at all. They know that bats eat thousands of pounds of mosquitoes and other insects every night.

Brush, Cacti, and Trees

No cowboy is properly dressed without a pair of chaps. Short for the Spanish word *chaparreras,* chaps are leather coverings worn over the pants. They're named for chapparal (thick brush)—a mix of brushy plants that includes spiny cacti, prickly mesquite, and thorny catclaws. Chapparal used to scratch cowboys' legs so badly that they began wearing chaps for protection.

Mesquite grows as either a shrub or a tree. It's a nuisance to cattle ranchers because it takes over grasslands, but Indians ate its high-protein beans and used its leaves as a medicine. Mesquite also makes sturdy furniture and good firewood. Mesquite-grilled meat is popular for its savory, smoky taste.

South Texas is brush country. Its arid soil supports short trees and tough shrubs and grasses. Yuccas, century plants, and creosote flourish in arid regions too. Century plants, also called American aloe, take many years to bloom (though rarely a hundred years!). Guayule (rubber plant) and candelilla (wax plant) are native to the far west.

Cacti are common in the south and west. More than 100 types of cactus grow in Texas—more than in all the rest of the United States. Prickly pear cacti are the most common in Texas. They yield a beautiful flower and a nourishing fruit. The pads, called *nopales* in Spanish, are eaten as a vegetable. Another species, the cholla cactus, grows long, thin "arms."

Outsiders picture Texas as they see it in Western movies—covered with deserts and plains. But about 15 percent of the state is forested. Tall pines grow in the Piney Woods of East Texas, as well as hardwoods such as oaks, hickory, and gum trees. Shorter trees grow west of the Piney Woods. Because post oak is common in this band of low forest, it's called the Post Oak Belt. Mixed in with the post oaks are blackjack oak, pecan, hickory, walnut, and elm trees.

Cypress trees

Uvalde bigtooth maples grow in the canyons of the Lost Maples area near Vanderpool in the Edwards Plateau. Also called canyon maples, these trees aren't lost—they're just picky about where they grow. They thrive only in protected sections of mountainous areas where the temperature, humidity, moisture, and sunlight are just right for their growth. Texas's forestry association has chosen the bigtooth maple as a State Champion Big Tree. Other state champs are a Texas ash and an Escarpment chokecherry.

Tall cypresses line the eastern riverbanks. These spindly-legged trees, with long roots growing aboveground, have been growing since the time of the dinosaurs. Tropical palm trees grow in the south along the Rio Grande. High in the mountains of West Texas are piñon and ponderosa pine, spruce, cedar, oak, and mesquite.

Grass once covered most of Texas. Overgrazing has thinned out the state's grasslands, but cattle still graze across millions of acres of Texas range. Besides feeding cattle, the grasses anchor the soil and prevent wind and water erosion.

More than 500 types of grass carpet the prairies and plains. The most common are bluestem, grama, buffalo grass, switchgrass, and Indiangrass. Tall marsh grasses grow in the swamps along the Gulf Coast.

Wildflowers

The bluebonnet, Texas's state flower, covers the roadsides with a blanket of blue in the spring. Early settlers gave it the name because its flowers look like sunbonnets. It's one of more than 5,000 wildflower species that grow in Texas. Other colorful species are Indian paintbrush, butterfly weed, primroses, black-eyed Susans, verbenas, phlox, goldenrod, and thistle.

Texas takes its wildflowers seriously. The highway department carefully plans and plants the roadsides with tons of wildflower seeds every year. Wildflower trails throughout the state offer especially beautiful views. In Austin, the Lady Bird Johnson Wildflower Center preserves and studies North America's native wildflowers, grasses, and other plants. It was founded by Claudia Taylor (Lady Bird) Johnson, widow of President Lyndon Johnson.

Fools and Strangers, Beware!

An old Texas saying goes, "Only fools and strangers predict the weather in Texas." The modern version tells the same tale: "If you don't like the weather, stick around—it'll change."

Summer brings the state's most dangerous weather. For tornado chasers, Texas is the place to be. It's the nation's top-ranking state in number of tornadoes per year. In 1995, 232 twisters touched down in Texas. There were 138 in 1996 and 191 in 1997. In the Panhandle,

A tornado near Pelican Island

hot summer winds whistle across the plains, bringing sandstorms and duststorms. Getting caught in one of these storms can be terrifying. The blowing dust is so thick that people can't see the sun—or anything else in any direction. And the wind can drive grains of sand so hard that they sting the skin like a thousand pinpricks.

Cities along the Gulf Coast have learned to be ready for hurricanes, too. A hurricane in 1900 destroyed the city of Galveston, killing more than 6,000 people. At the time, it was the worst weather disaster in U.S. history. Now a seawall shelters the city from gulf winds and waves, and hurricane warnings give people time to take cover or leave the area.

Texans expect to be hot in the summer. But no one predicted the heat wave that fried North Texas in the summer of 1998. For weeks on end, temperatures ranged well above 100°F (38°C). More than a hundred people died from heat-related causes.

Southern Texas is usually the state's warmest region. Its average January temperature is a pleasant 60°F (16°C), and July averages 85°F (29°C). Temperatures along the Gulf Coast are mild. Warm, moist air from the Gulf of Mexico keeps the area from being too hot in the summer and too cold in the winter.

Central Texas is mild year-round, while the northeastern woods are cool and wet. The Panhandle gets the state's coldest temperatures. In the winter, fierce winds called blue northers sweep down across the High Plains from the Rocky Mountains, bringing snow, sleet, and freezing rain. In less than an hour, the temperature can plunge 30°F (17°C).

On average, Texas skies are sunny for 248 days a year. But when sudden thunderstorms strike, creeks can swell to dangerous flood levels in no time. Southeast Texas receives the most rainfall, while the heaviest snows fall on the High Plains. The upper Panhandle averages 24 inches (60 cm) of snow a year. In January, blizzards may rage in the Panhandle, while the Rio Grande valley registers over 90°F (32°C). Brownsville, in the far south, has had no snow in the last hundred years.

CHAPTER SIX

So Much to See, So Much to Do

exas is too big to see in one trip. It's best to visit one or two regions at a time. Each new glimpse is a chance to enjoy more of the state's natural landscapes, wildlife, cowboy culture, Mexican flavor, big-city entertainment, and historic landmarks.

West Texas

The dry desert and jagged mountains of West Texas make perfect scenery for Western movies. Towns are few, and many residents drive an hour or more to reach a major shopping center.

El Paso is situated among high mountain peaks.

High peaks surround El Paso. Since ancient times, the site was a mountain pass—first for Indians, then for explorers and settlers. El Paso is so far west, it might as well be in New Mexico. It's closer to Santa Fe, the capital of New Mexico, than it is to Austin. While the rest of Texas is in the Central Time Zone, El Paso runs on Mountain Time.

El Paso is the mining, shopping, and cultural center for the far west. It's also the largest U.S. city on the Mexico border. It sits across from Ciudad Juárez, Mexico's largest border city.

Indians built El Paso's two missions—Ysleta and Socorro—in the 1680s. The Tigua Indian Reservation—Ysleta del Sur Pueblo—

Opposite: Hiking in Big Bend National Park

is the oldest community in Texas. At the Tigua Arts and Crafts Center, Native Americans perform traditional dances for the public and sell pottery, jewelry, wood carvings, and bread.

The El Paso Museum of History recreates the region's past with life-size scenes of Indians, explorers, and cavalrymen. The Border Patrol Museum displays uniforms, equipment, and documents from Texas's long history of guarding the border. Fort Bliss opened in 1848 to defend the area from Indians. Today it's the nation's largest army air defense center.

Four of the state's highest peaks rise in Guadalupe Mountains National Park, including Guadalupe Peak, the highest point in Texas. The mountains look dry and barren from a distance. But the park has pine forests, scenic canyons, and high meadows where deer and elk graze.

The town of Marfa is best known for the Marfa Lights, which appear every night in the desert sky just east of town. They move around, glow, split into two, and suddenly disappear. Even scientists agree that the lights are there, but no one can explain what they are.

Big Bend National Park rests in a "big bend" of the Rio Grande. It offers scenery and wildlife of three very different environments—deserts, mountains, and the Rio Grande. Visitors come to Big Bend for hiking, camping, horseback riding, river rafting, and bathing in the park's hot springs.

Terlingua, at the western edge of Big Bend, holds a chili cook-off every November. While people chow down the chili, musicians from the general store entertain them.

In the 1890s, Judge Roy Bean considered himself the "law

The site of the strange nighttime Marfa Lights

west of the Pecos." He dished out justice from Langtry, where the Pecos River meets the Rio Grande. Bean held court sessions in his saloon, which he named the Jersey Lily after British actress Lillie Langtry. Today, the Judge Roy Bean Visitor Center in Langtry preserves Bean's courtroom, billiard hall, and saloon.

Beneath west-central Texas lies the Permian Basin—a vast, underground "lake" of oil. The basin is responsible for much of the state's wealth and many of its wealthy people. Midland and Odessa are the region's major towns. Midland is the home of the Permian Basin Petroleum Museum, Library, and Hall of Fame. The University of Texas in Odessa holds a Shakespeare festival every year.

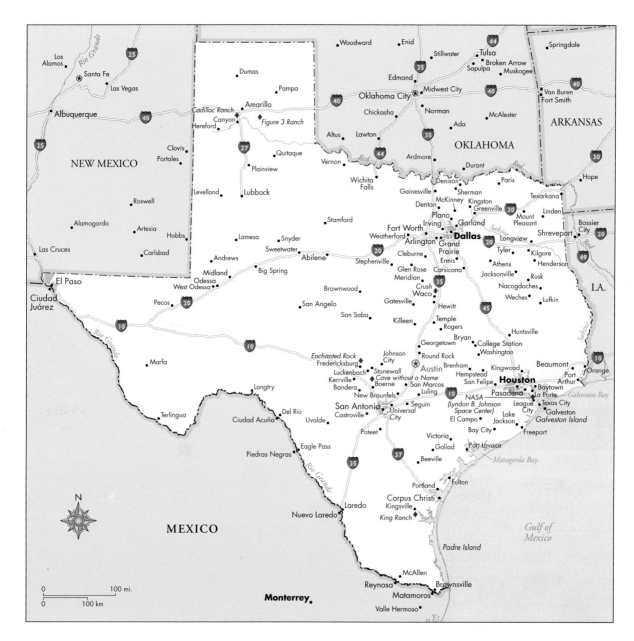

Texas's cities and interstates

The Panhandle

Amarillo, the largest city in the Panhandle, is a center for the region's cattle industry. Cattle auctions are held in the stockyards every week. Amarillo also has one of the world's largest helium plants.

In the summer, visitors can head out for a Cowboy Morning at the Figure 3 Ranch. The day begins with a big "cowboy breakfast" cooked over a campfire on the open range. A mule-drawn wagon ride and cattle roping and branding demonstrations fill out the day.

The Amarillo Museum of Art spreads out over three buildings on the Amarillo College campus. They were designed by Edward Stone, architect of the Kennedy Center in Washington, D.C.

The Cadillac Ranch, west of Amarillo, has the strangest "art" exhibit in Texas—a row of ten vintage Cadillacs buried nose-down in the sand with their tail fins pointing into the sky. They're positioned at exactly the same angle as the sides of the Great Pyramid of Cheops in Egypt. Helium magnate Stanley Marsh III installed the Cadillacs but never explained why.

Palo Duro Canyon, south of Amarillo, is called the Grand Canyon of Texas. A winding road leads from the canyon's rim down to its floor, 1,200 feet (366 m) below. At the bottom, people can explore the area by foot, on horseback, or aboard the Sad Monkey Railroad. On summer evenings, the musical *Texas* plays outdoors with the towering canyon walls in the background.

Hereford is called the "town without a toothache." Natural fluoride in the water supply keeps the residents' teeth from decaying. Hereford is also the home of the National Cowgirl Hall of Fame. It honors more than a hundred female rodeo champs and displays their riding costumes and trophies.

Caprock Canyons State Park near Quitaque features spectacular erosion-carved landscapes, colorful cliffs, and rugged canyons. It's a section of the Caprock Escarpment, marking the edge of the High Plains.

Palo Duro Canyon, known as the Grand Canyon of Texas

A bronze statue of rock-and-roll legend Buddy Holly stands in Lubbock, his birthplace. Around the statue is the Walk of Fame. Its bronze plaques honor other West Texas musicians such as Waylon Jennings, Roy Orbison, Jimmy Dean, and Tanya Tucker.

North-Central Texas

Abilene started out as a cattle-shipping railroad town, and cattle production is still one of its major industries. It was named after Abilene, Kansas, once the endpoint of the Chisholm Trail. The city celebrates its Old West heritage with both the West Texas Fair and the Western Heritage festival. Abilene's historic Grace Hotel now houses several museums: the Fine Arts Museum, the Abilene Historical Museum, and the Children's Museum. A brand-new addition is the national Center for Children's Illustrated Literature.

Outside the town stand the ruins of Fort Phantom. It was established in 1851 to protect settlers from Indians, but it was abandoned only three years later. Buffalo Gap Historic Village, south of Abilene, is a complex of twenty restored buildings from a frontier settlement.

Visitors to Dallas might not be able to tell they're in Texas. It's a modern city much like others around the United States, with steel-and-glass skyscrapers towering over the city center. Dallas is the headquarters for dozens of million-dollar companies and is one of the nation's top fashion-design centers. But, downtown Dallas does offer one big clue that this is Texas. In Pioneer Plaza, near city hall, three cowboys drive a herd of seventy Texas longhorn steers—all in bronze.

The downtown arts district sprawls over 60 acres (24 ha). Among its attractions are the Dallas Museum of Art, the Dallas Theater Center, and the Morton H. Meyerson Symphony Center. On the west side of town is the former Texas School Book Depository, where a gunman waited to shoot President John F. Kennedy. It's now a memorial museum called the Sixth Floor.

Riding the monorail is the best way to see the Wilds of Africa exhibit at the Dallas Zoo. The train sinks down to animal level for a better view of some of its ninety African species.

State Fair Park is the site of the Texas State Fair. But visitors

The Dallas Museum of Art is a main attraction in the downtown arts district.

come to the park the year-round to see the Dallas Aquarium, the Science Place museums, the Museum of Natural History, and the Hall of State history museum. The aquarium's Amazon Flooded Forest is a huge water tank teeming with fish of Brazil's Amazon River.

Thousands of gorgeous flowers, trees, and ferns cover the 66 acres (27 ha) of the Dallas Arboretum and Botanical Garden. Much of this land along White Rock Lake belonged to oilman Everett DeGolyer. His lavish mansion is now a museum.

Nearby Irving is the home of the Dallas Cowboys football team. It's also home to the largest horse sculpture in the world. The nine larger-than-life *Mustangs of Las Colinas* charge through a stream in Williams Square.

Fort Worth, just west of Dallas, was long known as a cow town. Cattle drives stopped there on their way to the railroad depots, and its stockyards were the largest in the world. For a feel of the Old West, visitors can hop aboard the Tarantula Railroad on Eighth Avenue. This 1896 steam engine chugs off to the Stockyards National Historic District, where boardwalks run along the Western-style shops and restaurants.

The city's famous museums include the Amon Carter Museum of Western Art, the Kimbell Art Museum, and the Modern Art Museum. A huge, curved screen surrounds viewers in the Omni Theater at the Museum of Science and History. Visitors can dig for dinosaur bones in the museum's DinoDig and see astronomy shows in the Noble Planetarium.

The Fort Worth Zoo is one of the best in the United States. Gorillas and other apes live in its tropical rain forest, and a rare white tiger roams through the Asian Falls habitat. Rhinoceroses and giraffes live in the African Savannah exhibit, and a Texas exhibit features prairie dogs and buffalo.

Lions are among the many animals that have homes in the Fort Worth Zoo.

Six Flags over Texas theme park is in Arlington, between Dallas and Fort Worth. Thrill seekers can ride a simulated jet as it breaks the sound barrier or take the Texas Giant, one of the tallest wooden roller coasters in the world. The park's Fun Sphere includes water bumper boats and a massive video arcade.

Some of the world's most endangered species live at the Fossil Rim Wildlife Center in Glen Rose, southwest of Dallas–Fort Worth. Bison, emus, and African oryxes are among the more than 1,100 animals that range over the center's 2,700 acres (1,093 ha) of savannah and woodland. The center also runs three-day safaris.

Dinosaur Valley State Park is another Glen Rose attraction. Gigantic dinosaurs left their tracks there 100 million years ago. Some footprints are the first tracks ever found of sauropods. These 60-foot (18-m) reptiles weighed 30 tons.

Farther north, toward the Oklahoma border, are Wichita Falls and Denison. Wichita Falls was named for a waterfall on the Wichita River, but the falls were flooded away in 1886. A century later, the city rebuilt the waterfall—ten times higher than the original. Denison is the birthplace of President Dwight D. Eisenhower.

East Texas

All four of Texas's national forests are in the Piney Woods of East Texas. Big Thicket National Preserve is a thick and swampy forest at the south end of the Piney Woods. Deer, foxes, wild hogs, and alligators roam through the lush preserve. Tall pines and cypresses loom overhead, and carnivorous (flesh-eating) pitcher plants grow in their shade. At the edge of Big Thicket is the Alabama-Coushatta Indian Reservation. Visitors can watch tribal ceremonies, eat tra-

Old Rip

Workers were just sealing up the cornerstone of the Eastland courthouse when a horned lizard jumped in. Thirty-one years later, in 1928, the courthouse was being torn down. People gathered around to watch as the old cornerstone was opened. Sure enough, there sat the critter—alive! He was named Old Rip, after Rip Van Winkle, and taken on tour around the country. Rip even traveled to Washington, D.C., where he visited President Calvin Coolidge.

Eleven months after his discovery, Old Rip died. His body rests in the new Eastland courthouse, in a velvet-lined coffin.

Skeptics of the tale say that "Rip" is a good name for the toad because it's short for "rip-off." At any rate, Old Rip's story inspired a famous Warner Brothers' cartoon about a singing, dancing frog. ■

ditional foods, and tour the swamp. Lufkin, in the heart of the Piney Woods, is home to the Museum of East Texas and the Texas Forestry Museum.

Tyler is called the Rose Capital of the World—more than half of the nation's commercial roses are grown there. Thousands of roses of every color can be seen at the Municipal Rose Garden, the Rose Museum, and Tyler's annual Texas Rose Festival.

Beaumont, Port Arthur, and Orange form a triangle in Texas's southeast corner. It was once called the Golden Triangle because of its oil industries.

Tyler is famous for its roses.

Now the area is best known as Cajun country. (Cajuns are descendants of the French Acadian colony that were transplanted from Louisiana.) Cajun foods such as crayfish and shrimp étoufée are at their best here.

Beaumont really came alive when the great Spindletop gusher burst forth in 1901. In no time, the little town became a city of 30,000 people. Gladys City Boomtown, on Beaumont's Lamar University campus, is a replica of the towns that sprang up overnight around the gusher.

Beaumont's Edison Plaza Museum displays several of Thomas Edison's inventions. At the Fire Museum of Texas, kids can check out antique fire engines. Beaumont also has a museum honoring local hero Babe Didrikson Zaharias, the Olympic gold medalist and golf champ.

The 1960s rock star Janis Joplin was born and raised in Port Arthur. She's one of the musicians honored in the Southeast Texas Musical Heritage Exhibit at Port Arthur's Museum of the Gulf Coast. Near Port Arthur are two wildlife refuges—McFaddin and Texas Point. They shelter more than 100,000 ducks and 60,000 snow geese. McFaddin's alligator population is one of the largest in the state.

The Gulf Coast

Galveston was the state's largest city in the 1800s. After the devastating hurricane of 1900, the city built a seawall for protection. Now people jog, bike, and stroll along the seawall, and hotels and beach houses overlook it. Galveston's ten-day Mardi Gras celebration is the year's biggest bash.

Carriage rides take sightseers through Galveston's historic districts—the Strand and the East End. They pass beautiful mansions such as Ashton Villa, the Williams Home, and the forty-two-room Moody Mansion. The Bishop's Palace is a work of art. It took sixty-one artisans seven years to carve its oak stairway. Trolley cars run from the Strand district to the beach.

Pirates, Karankawa Indians, and the hurricane are all part of the regional history that comes to life in the Galveston County Historical Museum. The square-rigged sailing ship *Elissa* is open for tours at the Texas Seaport Museum. At the Railroad Museum, visitors can board the Texas Limited, a restored train that runs between Galveston and Houston.

Galveston is a beautiful coastal town.

The Johnson Space Center

Rush-hour traffic in Houston is a fright. That's no surprise, since the vibrant city is the largest in Texas and the fourth-largest in the nation. Wealthy oilmen began running their operations from Houston in the early 1900s.

Since then, Houston has become a center for the aerospace industry, medical research, international banking and shipping, and high-tech manufacturing. In the 1960s, the Johnson Space Center brought in thousands of aerospace scientists and technicians. Today, Houston's Texas Medical Center is the world's largest medical complex. It employs more people than any other business in the city.

In downtown Houston, miles of air-conditioned pedestrian tunnels run beneath buildings, with shops and restaurants all along the way. Not far away, Old Market Square preserves dozens of historic buildings from the city's old downtown area. The Museum of Texas History reaches back even further. Exhibits range from sixteenth-century Spanish treasure to space exploration. The museum is part of Houston's 19-acre (7.7 ha) Sam Houston Memorial Park.

Arts buildings in the Civic Center showcase the Houston Symphony Orchestra, Grand Opera, and Ballet. Houston's Museum of Fine Arts features ancient Egyptian, Greek, and Roman art, as well as European paintings. Opened in 1924, it was the first art museum in Texas.

The Houston Zoo's tropical birdhouse is like an Asian jungle, with 200 exotic birds flying freely overhead. The zoo's rain forest for monkeys and large apes covers 2.2 acres (1 ha).

More than 1,500 butterflies flit through their habitat at the Houston Museum of Natural Science. Some of the most beautiful butterflies in the world land on visitors as they walk through. In the

Pioneers of the Heart

Texas has two world-famous surgeons who are pioneers in heart surgery. Dr. Michael DeBakey (left) was born in Louisiana in 1908. As a medical student, he invented a part of the heart-lung machine that made open-heart surgery possible. DeBakey began teaching at Baylor University's School of Medicine in 1948. In 1964, he performed the world's first coronary bypass operation, using a vein from the patient's leg.

Dr. Denton Cooley (right) was born in Houston in 1920. He studied at Johns Hopkins University and joined the faculty of Baylor University's School of Medicine in 1951.

Cooley was a pioneer in open-heart and heart-transplant surgery. He founded the Texas Heart Institute in Houston in 1962. In 1969, Cooley became the first surgeon to implant an artificial heart in a human. ■

museum's planetarium, people can take a virtual flight into a black hole or speed through constellations.

Space Center Houston is a great place to try on space gear, land a space shuttle, and see how an astronaut lives. The Disney-designed space museum is part of the Lyndon B. Johnson Space Center.

Corpus Christi is the state's most popular coastal city. Its warm weather and glistening beaches attract thousands of people every year. On Padre Island National Seashore, they stroll along the white-sand beach collecting seashells and driftwood that wash up

Thousands of people enjoy the beaches of Corpus Christi each year.

on shore. But anyone who loves peace and quiet knows to stay away from South Padre Island in the spring. Thousands of college students gather there for a rowdy time during spring break.

The Texas State Aquarium is just north of downtown Corpus Christi. Visitors enter through a glass tunnel with water cascading overhead. The aircraft carrier USS *Lexington* is docked nearby, and parks and picnic areas cover the whole area.

The Asian Cultures Museum holds the country's largest collection of handcrafted Japanese *hakata* dolls, with about thirty of them on display. The museum also offers flower-arranging classes and other educational programs.

Outside Corpus Christi is Aransas National Wildlife Refuge, the winter home for rare whooping cranes. Other wild residents are alligators, javelinas, and armadillos, as well as 400 species of birds. In Kingsville, southwest of Corpus Christi, is the massive King Ranch. It's the largest ranch in the continental United States. Tours lead to an old cow camp, historic cattle pens, and ranch headquarters. At the Texas Zoo in Victoria, wild animals of Texas roam in their natural habitats.

Central Texas

Westward-bound travelers used to ferry across the Brazos River at Waco. The crossing was much easier after a bridge was built in 1870. Once the longest suspension bridge in the world, the bridge is still open to pedestrians.

Two stars were born in Waco—the soft drink Dr Pepper and comedian Steve Martin. Dr Pepper began as a soda fountain drink at Waco's Old Corner Drug Store. The recipe today is almost the

The Texas Ranger Hall of Fame and Museum is located in Waco.

same as the original 1885 formula. Steve Martin's recipe for wacky comedy has turned him into a highly successful actor and director.

Waco's museums cover a lot of territory. The Texas Ranger Hall of Fame and Museum traces the history of the famous frontier lawmen. The Texas Sports Hall of Fame honors the state's many star athletes. And Dr Pepper's old bottling plant is now the Dr Pepper Museum. Baylor University's Armstrong-Browning Library holds all the original, handwritten poetry of Robert and Elizabeth Barrett Browning. Each of the fifty-four stained-glass windows in the elegant library illustrates one of their poems.

Modern, high-rise office buildings line Congress Avenue in Austin, the state capital. But Congress at Sixth Street belongs to another time. This historic district preserves dozens of Victorian- and Renaissance-style buildings, many from the 1850s. Farther up Sixth Street, music fans can hear country, rock, blues, and reggae every night in dozens of music clubs.

The capitol, built of native Texan pink granite, is the largest state capitol in the country. Atop its pink-painted metal dome is a statue of the Roman goddess of Liberty, Libertas. Inside, visitors can watch the legislature when it's in session.

Austin is situated on the Colorado River.

East of the capitol is the General Land Office, the oldest state office building in Texas. Now it's a visitors' center and history museum. The short-story writer O. Henry (William Sidney Porter) worked in this building before he became famous. West of the capitol is the governor's mansion, built in 1856. The French Legation Museum was the French embassy back in the days of the Texas Republic. Built in 1841, it is the oldest building in Austin.

About 50,000 students attend the University of Texas at Austin. It's the site of the Lyndon B. Johnson Presidential Library and Museum, the largest presidential library in the country. Displays highlight his Great Society programs, the Vietnam War, and other events of Johnson's term. Also on campus are the Huntington Art Gallery and the Ransom Humanities Research Center.

On the south edge of town, people can stroll, jog, or bike along trails around Town Lake. Town Lake is really a section of the Colorado River, which runs through town. In Zilker Park, southwest of downtown, a natural spring bubbles up to make a super-clean swimming pool. Other natural wonders burst forth at the Lady Bird

The Great Crash at Crush

More than 30,000 people gathered on the prairie at Crush, near Waco, on September 15, 1896. What was the attraction? A head-on collision of two 35-ton locomotives. The event was a publicity stunt organized by William George Crush, who had set up the "town" of Crush just for the occasion. One of the train's boilers exploded upon impact, hurling debris into the crowd. Two people were killed, including one man who was watching from up in a tree. ■

Johnson Wildflower Center, the nation's only institution devoted to native plants of North America.

At the Austin Children's Museum, kids can touch the exhibits and even climb on them. Bat fans can visit the world's largest urban bat colony hanging beneath the Congress Avenue Bridge over Town Lake. Sightseers gather at dusk to watch more than a million bats swoop out from their roosts.

The Hill Country

The Hill Country rises west of Austin and north of San Antonio. It's a region of small towns, hilly pastures, and natural springs. German, Czech, Polish, and Scots-Irish immigrants settled the Hill Country, and their culture lives on in many of the towns.

Many residents of Fredericksburg still speak German. Throughout the year, the town celebrates German festivals such as Oktoberfest, Easter Fires, Kristkindl Market, and Kinderfest. The octagonal Vereins Kirche (People's Church) stands in the old town square. The original church was the town's first public building, and this rebuilt version is now a museum. The Admiral Nimitz Museum is named for the U.S. Pacific fleet commander, who was born there. It includes a World War II museum and a Japanese peace garden.

North of town is Enchanted Rock, a massive pink-granite dome that covers about 640 acres (259 ha). Prehistoric people held it sacred, and Native Americans believed it was a dwelling place for spirits. Campers might agree when they hear the mountain "groan" at night. It's the sound of the granite contracting in the cool air after a day in the hot sun.

"Ain't nobody feelin' no pain" in Luckenbach, says a Willie Nelson and Waylon Jennings song. Ain't nobody livin' there, either—at least, not many. Luckenbach's official population is twenty-five. But thousands come to Willie's annual Fourth of July picnic for an all-day concert.

President Lyndon B. Johnson's ancestors settled Johnson City. Today, a national historic park encompasses Johnson's boyhood home, as well as his grandfather's rustic cabin and stone farm buildings.

Texans spend time hiking, camping, and rock climbing at Enchanted Rock State Natural Area.

The Camel Cavalry

Jefferson Davis is best known as the president of the Confederate States of America during the Civil War (1861–1865). Before then, as U.S. secretary of war, Davis imported camels to carry supplies across the desert of southwest Texas. The camels were stationed at Kerrville in central Texas. From there, they trekked west through the Davis Mountains, New Mexico, and Arizona to Fort Yuma, California. ■

The rugged hills and green valleys near Kerrville are full of children's summer camps. Adults come for the healthful dry climate and dude ranches. Photographers like to snap pictures of the exotic wild animals on the Wilson-Haley Ranch. In town, some of the attractions are the Cowboy Artists of America Museum and the Hill Country Museum.

Polish immigrants founded Bandera. They built St. Stanislaus Catholic Church there in 1876, and it's still an active parish. The U.S. Army's camel corps was stationed at Camp Verde in the 1850s.

Boerne is the site of the Cave without a Name. In 1939, a little boy won the contest to name the cave when he said, "This cave is too pretty to name." Stalagmites, stalactites, and other formations grow from its floor, ceiling, and walls. Nearby Cascade Caverns has a magnificent underground waterfall and sparkling crystal pools.

Near New Braunfels is Natural Bridge Caverns, an awesome underground maze of gigantic rooms and corridors. The Hummel Museum in town displays hundreds of Sister M. I. Hummel's paintings and drawings of rosy-cheeked children, and porcelain figurines based on her artwork.

South Texas

San Antonio sits between the Hill Country to the north and brush-covered plains to the south. The city was founded as a Spanish mission in 1718. Now that mission is known as the Alamo, Texas's most famous historical site.

Mexican influence is strong in San Antonio, and Mexican holidays are bright and festive, with lively music, colorful costumes, and delicious food. The downtown shopping area re-creates

A festival at Mission
San José in San Antonio

San Antonio's old Mexican flavor. The ten-room Spanish Governor's Palace was once the seat of Spanish government in Texas. The King William Historic District preserves mansions built by German merchants in the 1870s.

San Antonio's El Mercado is much like a typical Mexican marketplace. Local merchants sell handcrafted pottery, wood carvings, and leather goods, as well as fresh fruit and vegetables.

The San Antonio River winds through downtown, and the *Paseo del Rio* (River Walk) runs alongside it. The walk goes on for miles, lined with sidewalk cafés, boutiques, restaurants, and hotels. Visitors can also take a riverboat ride to see it all.

Besides the Alamo site, San Antonio has four other missions. Mission San José, known as the Queen of the Missions, is the largest and best restored of them all. Ornately sculpted stone surrounds the church's front entry and south window, called Rosa's

San Antonio's River Walk

Window. The complex includes Indian residences, a convent, a flour mill, a granary, and an outdoor stone oven.

Several military bases operate in the area, and most of them welcome visitors. Fort Sam Houston is the army headquarters for a five-state area. On site are a military museum and an army medical museum. San Antonio's four air force bases are Brooks, Kelly, Lackland, and Randolph.

The town of Washington was Washington-on-the-Brazos in its days of glory. Revolutionaries signed the Texas Declaration of Independence there, and it was the Texas Republic's capital. The Star of the Republic Museum presents the everyday life, politics, and military events of that time.

The fertile Rio Grande valley stretches across the state's southern tip. With Mexico just across the Rio Grande, Mexican influences are strong there. In border towns, the smell of spicy Mexican food and the sounds of Spanish guitar drift on the air.

People who live in cooler climates like to spend winter vacations in this sunny valley. Tropical flowers and palm trees line the streets, and roadside stands sell fresh vegetables and citrus fruits. Most visitors cross the border into Mexico for a day of shopping, eating, and sightseeing. Matamoros (across from Brownsville) and Nuevo Laredo (across from Laredo) are favorite destinations.

Laredo is the major international crossing point along the border. It has the nation's largest inland port, and much of the city revolves around importing and exporting. Laredo is also the most Mexican of the border towns. More than 90 percent of the residents are Mexican, and most speak both Spanish and English.

Brownsville is Texas's southernmost city and the largest city in the Rio Grande valley. Industries include electronics, automotive assembly, and shipping from its international seaport. Downtown signs are in Spanish and English, or in Spanish alone. Charro Days is the major event of the year. Held in February, it's a four-day, two-nation fiesta, parade, and carnival.

Jaguars, kangaroos, tigers, and gorillas roam in their natural habitats at Brownsville's Gladys Porter Zoo. Named one of the ten best zoos in America, it's home to more than 1,500 animals from Asia, Africa, Australia, and tropical South America. Outside the city is the Santa Ana National Wildlife Refuge—a home for rare birds and other animals found nowhere else in the United States.

CHAPTER SEVEN

The Power of the People

"All political power," says the Texas state constitution, "is inherent in the people. . . . They have at all times the inalienable right to alter, reform, or abolish their government in such manner as they think expedient."

This rugged, freedom-loving spirit has been part of Texans' outlook since the first settlers arrived. The Republic of Texas adopted its constitution in 1836. As a state, Texas drew up new constitutions in 1845, 1861, 1866, 1869, and 1876. The 1876 constitution still stands today. But citizens can "alter, reform, or abolish" it through amendments, or changes. Once the legislature has approved a constitutional amendment, citizens have the final word. It takes only a simple majority—more than half of those who vote—to pass the amendment.

Many Texans believe their constitution is too narrow-minded for modern times. Voters have added more than 200 amendments since 1876. In 1974, a constitutional convention met to draw up a new constitution, However, the members couldn't agree on what should be in it. Citizens clearly wanted a change, though. The next year, they approved a total of eight new amendments.

Texas's legislative chambers

Opposite: The capitol in Austin

The governor's mansion

Texas's state government is organized just like the U.S. government. Power is divided three ways to make sure there's always a balance of power. The three divisions of state government are the executive, legislative, and judicial branches.

The Executives

The executive branch of government makes sure the state's laws are carried out. Texas's governor is the head of the executive branch and the state's chief executive officer. Voters can elect a governor to as many four-year terms as they wish. The governor can propose laws to the legislature, veto laws that have passed, call special legislative sessions, and appoint the secretary of state and other officials.

In Texas, a governor is not as powerful as governors in some other states. That's because so many high executive officials are elected, instead of appointed. Voters elect the lieutenant governor, attorney general, and comptroller, as well as the heads of several important state commissions and agencies. This sometimes makes it hard for a governor to put his or her policies into effect statewide. On the other hand, a governor who has strong leadership abilities can win the support of both the legislature and the public.

The Lawmakers

The state legislature holds the legislative, or lawmaking, power. Like the U.S. Congress, Texas's legislature is bicameral, or made up of two houses—the 31-member senate and the 150-member house

Texas governor George W. Bush, son of former president George Bush.

Sam Rayburn

Samuel Taliaferro Rayburn (1882–1961) was one of the country's most influential politicians. A Texas resident since age five, he became a powerful Democrat in Texas's house of representatives (1907–1912). Joining the U.S. House of Representatives in 1913, he served as Speaker of the House for many years (1940–1946, 1949–1953, 1955–1961). Rayburn's influence covered a wide range. He sponsored New Deal programs during the depression, encouraged the establishment of the United Nations, and supported President John F. Kennedy's liberal policies. ■

The State Flag and Seal

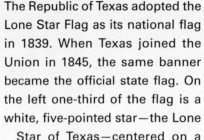

The Republic of Texas adopted the Lone Star Flag as its national flag in 1839. When Texas joined the Union in 1845, the same banner became the official state flag. On the left one-third of the flag is a white, five-pointed star—the Lone Star of Texas—centered on a field of blue. On the right are two horizontal stripes—a white stripe on the top and a red stripe on the bottom. As in the U.S. flag, the Stars and Stripes, blue represents loyalty, white stands for strength, and red is for bravery.

Texas's state seal is based on the five-pointed star used as the emblem for the Republic of Texas, created in 1836. Since that time, many versions of the star have been used on official documents. In 1991, John Hannah Jr., Texas's secretary of state, decided to form a single design for the seal. The current seal has a front and back, but the reverse is used for decorative purposes only. ■

Texas's State Symbols

State bird: Mockingbird Mockingbirds mimic the songs of other birds. They repeat a call over and over, then quickly jump to another bird's song. One mockingbird may know twenty-five or more different bird songs. Adult mockingbirds are light gray with a white breast and a long tail. They fiercely protect their nests, often dive-bombing people or animals that venture too close. The popular mockingbird is also the state bird of Arkansas, Florida, Mississippi, and Tennessee.

State small mammal: Armadillo The armadillo is an insect-eating mammal about the size of a cat. Its bony shell protects it from predators. Native to South America, armadillos now live as far north as Kansas. They dig burrows in the ground and are also good at digging for grub worms—one of their favorite foods. They cannot live in areas where the ground is too hard to dig. In March, a mother armadillo goes into her burrow and has four babies—all the same sex.

State insect: Monarch butterfly Monarch butterflies are the only butterflies that migrate when the seasons change, instead of hibernating. It takes about a month for a monarch to go through its three stages of life. It hatches from the egg as a yellow-and-white striped caterpillar. Next, it spins a chrysalis, or case, around itself. Finally, the black and orange butterfly emerges from the chrysalis.

State flower: Bluebonnet Bluebonnets (above right) bloom across central and southern Texas in the early spring. Settlers in the 1800s gave this blue wildflower its name. They thought it looked like a woman's sunbonnet. Some other names for the bluebonnet are lupine, buffalo clover, wolf flower, and *el conejo* (jackrabbit).

State tree: Pecan Pecan trees are native to North America. They can grow up to 150 feet (46 m) or more. Their nuts are brown, usually with black streaks and are often used in pies, cookies, brownies, and other delicious foods. Texas is the nation's largest producer of pecans. Governor James Hogg liked pecan trees so much that he asked that one be planted over his grave. The oldest known pecan tree is in Weatherford, Texas. Its trunk measures 19 feet 2 inches (5.8 m) around.

State plant: Prickly pear cactus The prickly pear (below right) is Texas's most common cactus. Its fruit is made into jelly, and its pads are eaten as a vegetable.

State gemstone: Blue topaz Topaz occurs naturally in many colors, including blue, orange, green, pink, and red. When treated with radiation, colorless topaz turns various shades of blue.

Texas's State Song
"Texas, Our Texas"

After a statewide contest, Texas legislators voted to adopt "Texas, Our Texas" in 1929. The words are by Gladys Y. Wright and William J. Marsh, and the music is by William J. Marsh.

Texas, Our Texas! all hail the
  mighty State!
Texas, Our Texas! so wonder-
  ful, so great!
Boldest and grandest, with-
  standing ev'ry test
O Empire wide and glorious,
  you stand supremely blest.

Chorus:
God bless you Texas! And keep
  you brave and strong,
That you may grow in power
  and worth, throughout the
  ages long.
God bless you Texas! And keep
  you brave and strong,
That you may grow in power
  and worth, throughout the
  ages long.

Texas, O Texas! your freeborn
  single star,
Sends out its radiance to
  nations near and far,
Emblem of Freedom! it set our
  hearts aglow,

With thoughts of San Jacinto
  and glorious Alamo.

(Chorus)

Texas, dear Texas! from tyrant
  grip now free,
Shines forth in splendor, your
  star of destiny!
Mother of heroes, we come
  your children true,
Proclaiming our allegiance,
  our faith, our love for you.

(Chorus)

of representatives. Voters in each of the state's 31 senatorial districts elect one senator to a four-year term. The 150 representative districts elect their members to two-year terms.

The lawmakers meet in the state capitol in Austin. Regular sessions begin on the second Tuesday in January of every other year. The governor may call a special session if there is urgent business to discuss. The lieutenant governor presides over the senate. In the house, representatives elect one of their members to be speaker of the house.

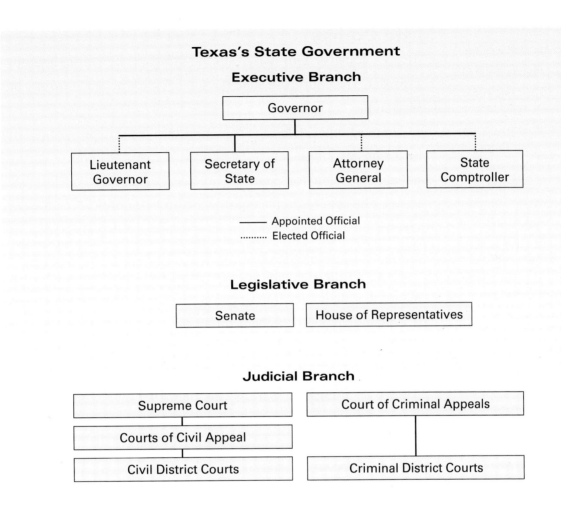

Texas's State Government

Executive Branch

Governor

Lieutenant Governor

Secretary of State

Attorney General

State Comptroller

——— Appointed Official
········· Elected Official

Legislative Branch

Senate

House of Representatives

Judicial Branch

Supreme Court

Court of Criminal Appeals

Courts of Civil Appeal

Civil District Courts

Criminal District Courts

Being a state legislator can be a good way to launch a career in politics. Many of Texas's legislators have gone on to become famous national figures. As a young man, Sam Rayburn was the speaker of the house in Texas's legislature. Later in life, he was speaker of the U.S. House of Representatives for seventeen of his forty-nine years as a U.S. congressman.

Lyndon Johnson

Lyndon Baines Johnson (1908–1973), born near Stonewall, was the thirty-sixth president of the United States. Trained as a school-teacher, he served in the U.S. House of Representatives (1937–1949) and the U.S. Senate (1949–1961). He was elected John F. Kennedy's vice president in 1960 and became president when Kennedy was assassinated in 1963. After winning the 1964 election, Johnson vigorously promoted his Great Society programs against poverty and racism. They included the Civil Rights Act (1964), the Voting Rights Act (1965), and social programs such as Medicare. His popularity slipped as he involved the country more deeply in the Vietnam War. In 1969, Johnson retired to his Texas ranch. ■

The Courts

Texas's court system makes up the judicial branch of state government. The courts use state laws to decide whether someone has broken the law.

In most other states, the supreme court is the highest court. But Texas has two high courts. For criminal cases, the court of criminal appeals is the top court. Its nine judges are elected to six-year terms. The state supreme court is the highest court for civil cases. Its chief justice and eight associate justices are also elected to six-year terms.

Both of these courts are known as courts of last resort. This means that their decisions are final. Cases come to the high courts if a defendant appeals a decision made in a lower court.

Beneath the top level, Texas has fourteen courts of civil appeal and 370 civil district courts. Most serious cases begin in a district court. For minor cases, trials take place in county, municipal, or justice-of-the-peace courts.

Local Government

Texas is divided into 254 counties—more than any other state. Brewster County, in the far west, is the largest. It could hold the entire state of Connecticut, with room to spare.

Counties are governed by a commissioners' court, made up of a county judge and four commissioners. Every county is divided into four precincts, each of which elects one of the commissioners. In spite of its name, the commissioners' court is not a trial court. It conducts such tasks as making county budgets and deciding on tax rates.

Texas's Governors

Name	Party	Term	Name	Party	Term
J. Pinckney Henderson	Dem.	1846–1847	S. W. T. Lanham	Dem.	1903–1907
George T. Wood	Dem.	1847–1849	Oscar B. Colquitt	Dem.	1911–1915
P. Hansborough Bell	Dem.	1849–1853	James E. Ferguson	Dem.	1915–1917
Elisha M. Pease	Dem.	1853–1857	William P. Hobby	Dem.	1917–1921
Hardin R. Runnels	Dem.	1857–1859	Pat M. Neff	Dem.	1921–1925
Sam Houston	Ind.	1859–1861	Miriam A. Ferguson	Dem.	1925–1927
Francis R. Lubbock	Dem.	1861–1863	Dan Moody	Dem.	1927–1931
Pendleton Murrah	Dem.	1863–1865	Ross Sterling	Dem.	1931–1933
Under federal military rule		1865	Miriam A. Ferguson	Dem.	1933–1935
Andrew J. Hamilton	Con.*	1865–1866	James V. Allred	Dem.	1935–1939
James W. Throckmorton	Con.*	1866–1867	W. Lee O'Daniel	Dem.	1939–1941
Elisha M. Pease	Rep.	1867–1869	Coke R. Stevenson	Dem.	1941–1947
Under federal military rule		1869–1870	Beauford H. Jester	Dem.	1947–1949
Edmund J. Davis	Rep.	1870–1874	Allan Shivers	Dem.	1949–1957
Richard Coke	Dem.	1874–1876	Price Daniel	Dem.	1957–1963
Richard B. Hubbard	Dem.	1876–1879	John B. Connally	Dem.	1963–1969
Oran M. Roberts	Dem.	1879–1883	Preston Smith	Dem.	1969–1973
John Ireland	Dem.	1883–1887	Dolph Briscoe	Dem.	1973–1979
Lawrence S. Ross	Dem.	1887–1891	Bill Clements	Rep.	1979–1983
James S. Hogg	Dem.	1891–1895	Mark White	Dem.	1983–1987
Charles A. Culberson	Dem.	1895–1899	Bill Clements	Rep.	1987–1991
Joseph D. Sayers	Dem.	1899–1903	Ann W. Richards	Dem.	1991–1995
Thomas M. Campbell	Dem.	1907–1911	George W. Bush	Rep.	1995–

* Confederate state governors

Cities with a population of 5,000 or more may choose to have home rule. That is, they may draw up their own charter, or body of laws. More than 200 cities in Texas have chosen this option. They elect a city council and either a city manager or a mayor. Smaller towns are ruled under general Texas law.

Texas's counties

Texas Leaders

Dwight D. Eisenhower

Dwight David Eisenhower (1890–1969), born in Denison, was the thirty-fourth president of the United States (1953–1961). During World War II, he commanded all Allied troops in Europe and led the D-Day invasion of Normandy, France. While he was president, he established the U.S. Air Force Academy.

John Nance Garner

John Nance Garner (1868–1967), known as Cactus Jack, was born in Red River County. He was speaker of the U.S. House of Representatives from 1931 to 1933 and vice president under President Franklin D. Roosevelt from 1933 to 1941.

Ann Richards

Democratic governor Ann Richards took office in 1991. She had previously been the state treasurer. Vivacious and outspoken, Richards gained nationwide attention with her "Where Was George?" speech at the 1992 Democratic National Convention. The convention nominated presidential candidate Bill Clinton, who went on to defeat Republican—and Texan—George Bush. Ironically, it was Bush's son, George W. Bush, who defeated Richards in the next governor's race.

George Bush

George Herbert Walker Bush (1924–) was the forty-first president of the United States (1989–1993). While living in Houston, he was an executive of the Zapata Offshore Company. He served as a U.S. congressman (1967–1971), director of the Central Intelligence Agency (1976–1977), and vice president under Ronald Reagan (1981–1989).

Barbara Jordan

Barbara C. Jordan (1936–1996), born in Houston, was the first African-American woman from the South to serve in the U.S. House of Representatives (1973–1979). Known for her powerful and eloquent speaking style, she delivered the keynote address at the 1976 Democratic National Convention. She also spoke out in the Richard Nixon impeachment hearings. ■

Democrats: No Longer a Slam Dunk

Texans elected Democratic governors for 105 years—from 1874 to 1979. Texas has usually supported Democrats for president, too. Before 1972, the state went for Republican presidential candidates only three times in its history.

Things have been changing since the 1970s, though. Texas gave its electoral votes to Republican presidential candidates Richard Nixon (1972), Ronald Reagan (1980 and 1984), and George Bush (1988 and 1992). In the governor's race, Republican William Clements finally broke the Democrats' winning streak in 1979. Another Republican, George W. Bush, took the governor's seat in 1995.

A Questionable Distinction

Texas is proud to have the "biggest" and the "most" of many things. But in one record-breaking area, Texans' feelings are seriously mixed. Texas has been called the "capital of capital punishment" because the state has executed more than 140 people since 1982. A record thirty-seven executions took place in 1997 alone. Both human rights groups and religious leaders have appealed for a change in Texas's death-penalty laws.

Some Texans have been changing their minds about the death penalty. Public support dropped to a low of 68 percent in 1998. That was the year when thirty-eight-year-old Karla Faye Tucker was executed for taking part in a brutal double murder. She was the first woman executed in Texas since the Civil War. Tucker drew worldwide attention because she was a woman and because she had embraced Christianity while in prison.

Tucker's case made Texans, and the entire country, reexamine some old questions. How important is it if death-row inmates turn their lives around? In a statewide poll, 31 percent of Texans said that a reformed prisoner should not be put to death. Does the death penalty really keep people from committing crimes? Only 50 percent of Texans believe that it does. Is there a good alternative to the death penalty? Many would prefer to sentence criminals to life imprisonment. The debate will surely continue, as more than 400 inmates wait on death row today.

CHAPTER EIGHT

Making a Living

Ranching continues to be an important way of life in Texas.

Texas has one of the largest economies in the world. Its gross state product (GSP) is more than half a *trillion* dollars. (The GSP is the value of all the goods and services the state produces in a year.) That outstrips the production of many entire countries.

Manufacturing, mining, and farming are huge industries in Texas, but service industries account for about 70 percent of the state's wealth. Texas's service workers include doctors, teachers, salespeople, bank tellers, real estate dealers, bus drivers, and state park employees. A hundred years ago, most Texans worked on farms or ranches.

Manufacturing

Texas's first factories turned farm products into many usable goods. Cotton was made into thread, cloth, and cottonseed oil. Wheat went to flour mills, and fruits and vegetables went to canning plants. Meatpacking plants opened after the Civil War. They had no refrigeration, so the meat was salted or pickled to preserve it. Tanneries made hides into leather.

Food processing is still big business in Texas. Grain, beef, fruit and vegetables, chickens, and milk are processed, packaged, and shipped all over the world. Soft drinks, beer, and other beverages

Opposite: The catch off Padre Island

are among the top processed foods. Most come from plants in Houston, Fort Worth, and San Antonio.

If someone took away all the petrochemicals from your life, you might not have much left. Petrochemicals are materials made from petroleum. Most plastics are petrochemicals. So are synthetic fabrics such as nylon. The pipes that bring water into your bathroom and kitchen are probably made of a petrochemical called polyvinyl chloride (PVC). Read the label on any bottle of shampoo or salad dressing. Ingredients with "ethylene" or "propylene" in the name are petrochemicals.

Chemicals are Texas's leading factory goods, and petrochemicals are the most valuable. Thousands of products are made from petroleum and natural gas, including explosives, cosmetics, paint, ink, drugs, pesticides, and fertilizers. Most of Texas's chemical plants are located in cities along the Gulf Coast, such as Houston, Corpus Christi, and Beaumont.

Transportation equipment is another top factory item. The most important are airplanes and aerospace equipment, made mainly in the Dallas–Fort Worth area. Texas factories also make mobile homes, trailers, ships, and boats. Automotive assembly plants are a big part of the manufacturing scene, too. They take car and truck parts made somewhere else and put them together. Many of the state's assembly plants are in towns along the Mexican border.

Texas also manufactures oil-field and farm machinery and electrical and electronic equipment. Texas Instruments makes specialized computer chips for many electronic devices. With all these modern industries, Texas's image of the Old West remains. Tanneries still make cowhide into leather for handcrafted cowboy boots, belts, chaps, and saddlebags.

The 1993 North American Free Trade Agreement (NAFTA) made it easier for Mexico, the United States, and Canada to carry on trade. Today Texas exports over $20 billion worth of goods to Mexico.

Johnson Space Center

The Lyndon B. Johnson Space Center is located in Clear Lake, near Houston. More than 15,000 engineers, scientists, astronauts, and technical specialists work there. Guided tours through this 1,620-acre (656-ha) facility give a close look at manned space flight. Space Center Houston (above) is in the main visitors' center. This spectacular education and entertainment complex features moon capsules, space-flight training devices, astronaut suits, and big-screen films. Visitors can practice landing a shuttle or retrieving a satellite. They can even take part in demonstrations that show how astronauts eat, sleep, and live. ■

Howard Hughes

Howard Robard Hughes (1905–1976), born in Houston, was a billionaire who made his fortune leasing oil-drilling equipment. In the 1930s, he became a Hollywood film producer and turned actresses Jean Harlow and Jane Russell into stars. An avid aviator, Hughes broke speed records and invented a wooden airplane called the *Spruce Goose*. His Hughes Aircraft Company and Las Vegas real estate investments added more millions to his wealth. In his later years, Hughes withdrew from society and saw only a few close friends. ■

Oil, Gas, and Other Minerals

Oil was discovered in Nacogdoches as early as 1866. But the state's petroleum industry really took off in 1901, when Beaumont's Spindletop gusher exploded. Within a year, hundreds of oil companies sprang up. Some of them grew to become today's Mobil, Exxon, Texaco, and Chevron companies.

With the discovery of the East Texas oil field in 1930, oil production really took off. Texas has led the nation in mineral production since 1935. About one-third of all the nation's petroleum lies below Texas soil.

What Texas Grows, Manufactures, and Mines

Agriculture	Manufacturing	Mining
Beef cattle	Chemicals	Natural gas
Corn	Electrical equipment	Petroleum
Cotton	Food products	
Sheep	Machinery	
Sorgham	Metal products	
	Transportation equipment	

The richest reserves are in the Permian Basin, an underground region in west-central Texas. But more than two-thirds of the state's land is sitting on top of oil. Pumps are extracting oil in the Panhandle, in South and East Texas, and offshore in the gulf tidelands. Texas plants refine the oil into a usable fuel and process it into chemicals.

Texas is also the number-one state in natural gas. One-third of all the natural gas used in the United States comes from Texas. Gigantic pipelines carry the gas as far away as New York City.

Oil and gas are just part of Texas's mineral wealth. After fuels,

H. L. Hunt

Oilman Haroldson Lafayette Hunt (1889–1974) was one of the richest men in the world. Born in Illinois, he spent the 1920s drilling for oil in Arkansas, Oklahoma, and Louisiana. After acquiring the first East Texas oil site, he founded the Dallas-based Hunt Oil Company in 1936. It became the country's largest independent oil company. Hunt was known for his ultraconservative political views. ■

Refining Texas Crude

Crude oil, pumped straight from the ground, is not very useful. It's made up of thousands of different chemical compounds. It has to be refined, or separated, into its many components. Under heat and other treatments, crude oil yields butane, gasoline, jet fuel, asphalt, waxes, and other substances. Most of Texas's oil refineries are located along the Gulf Coast. ■

the most valuable minerals are sand and gravel, crushed stone, and limestone. They are used in making concrete and in building roads. As Texas's industry and population grow, there's a strong demand for these materials. Texas also leads the nation in magnesium, a metal extracted from seawater. The state is also a top producer of sulphur, helium, and gypsum.

Cattle and Crops

Real cowboys still round 'em up in Texas, and about 15 million cattle live there. The best breeds are Texas longhorns and Santa Gertrudis. Longhorns came to Texas with the first Spanish explorers in Mexico. Some escaped and ran wild until Texas ranchers began rounding them up. Longhorns are a tough breed that survives extreme weather and resists disease. Breeders on the King Ranch crossed shorthorns and Brahmans to produce the Santa Gertrudis breed.

Mohair is a silky-feeling wool spun from the fleece of Angora goats. Almost all the mohair in the United States comes from the Angora goats that graze the Texas hills. More sheep and goats live in Texas than in any other state.

Cotton has been Texas's main crop for most of its his-

About 15 million cattle are raised in Texas.

King Ranch

King Ranch, southwest of Corpus Christi, is the biggest ranch in the continental United States. It's also the world's largest privately owned ranch. It stretches over four counties, covering more than 825,000 acres (334,000 ha).

Richard King, a steamboat captain, started the ranch in 1853. The King family developed the Santa Gertrudis breed of cattle at their ranch and bred many champion racehorces.

Visitors can tour the ranch, trace its history in the King Ranch Museum, and shop for leather goods at the King Ranch Saddle Shop.

tory. Even today, Texas is the nation's top cotton grower. About one-third of the state's farmland is devoted to crops. Texas ranks second in the country in sorghum, peanuts, blackeyed peas, and honeydews. It's the number-three state for cabbage, celery, cucumbers, spinach, watermelons, navel oranges, and grapefruit. Texas farmers also grow chili peppers, pears, apples, and blueberries.

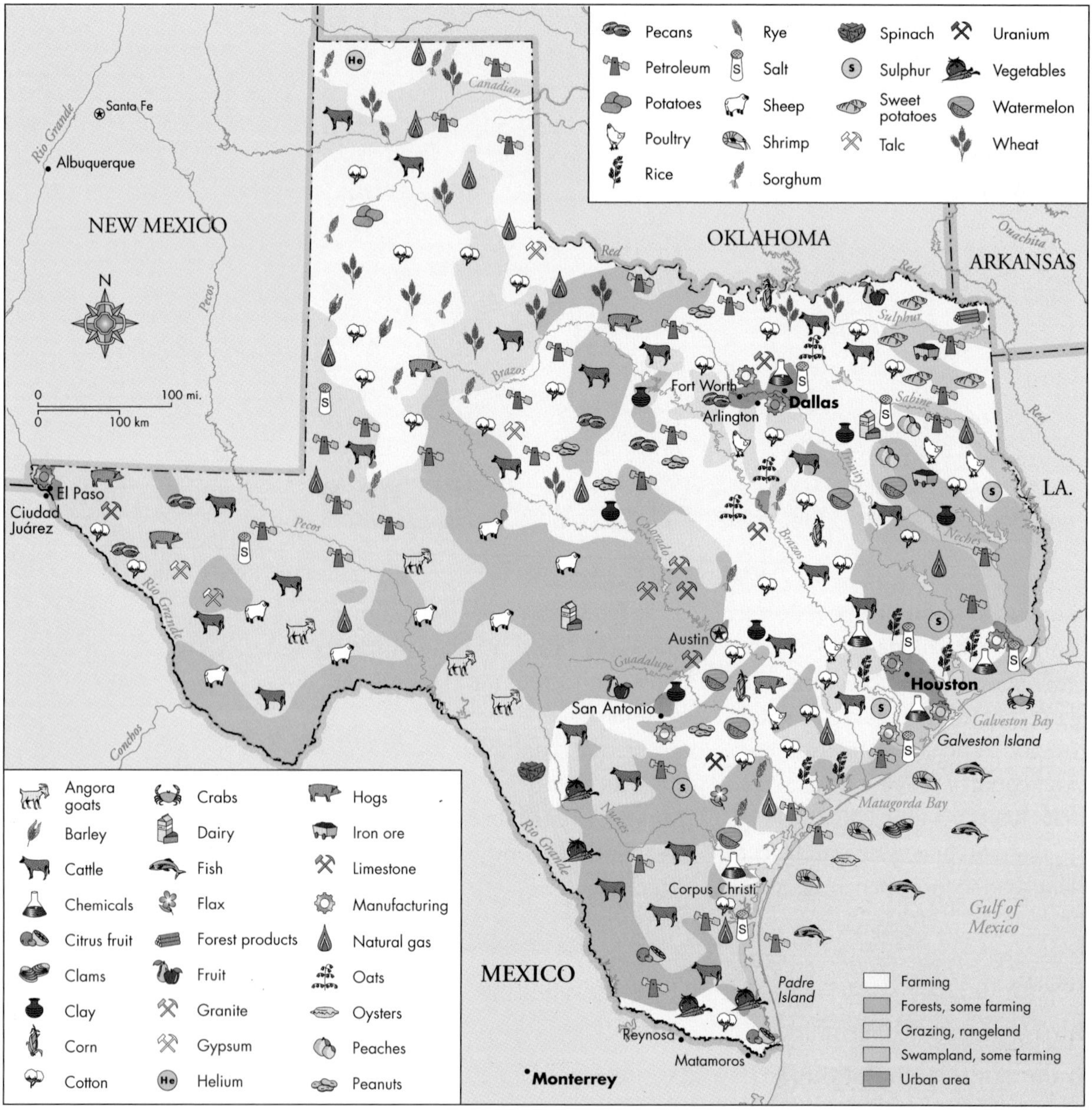
NEW MEXICO
Santa Fe
Albuquerque
Rio Grande
Pecos
Canadian
N
0 100 mi.
0 100 km
OKLAHOMA
ARKANSAS
Ouachita
Red
Sulphur
Sabine
LA.
Fort Worth
Dallas
Arlington
Brazos
Trinity
Neches
Colorado
Austin
Guadalupe
San Antonio
Houston
Galveston Bay
Galveston Island
Matagorda Bay
Nueces
Corpus Christi
Gulf of Mexico
Padre Island
MEXICO
Reynosa
Matamoros
Monterrey
El Paso
Ciudad Juárez
Conchos
Pecans
Petroleum
Potatoes
Poultry
Rice
Rye
Salt
Sheep
Shrimp
Sorghum
Spinach
Sulphur
Sweet potatoes
Talc
Uranium
Vegetables
Watermelon
Wheat
Angora goats
Barley
Cattle
Chemicals
Citrus fruit
Clams
Clay
Corn
Cotton
Crabs
Dairy
Fish
Flax
Forest products
Fruit
Granite
Gypsum
Helium
Hogs
Iron ore
Limestone
Manufacturing
Natural gas
Oats
Oysters
Peaches
Peanuts
Farming
Forests, some farming
Grazing, rangeland
Swampland, some farming
Urban area

Texas's natural resources

Fresh fruits and vegetables grow in Texas all year-round. Winter gardens are at their best in the lower Rio Grande valley and the area around Laredo and Eagle Pass. The valley is known for its juicy grapefruits and oranges—Ruby Red grapefruit is the state fruit. Texas is also a leader in organic farming—raising crops without chemical fertilizers and pesticides.

Texas grows flowers, too. Poinsettias from the warm Rio Grande valley are shipped all over the country at Christmastime. Tyler, Texas's rose capital, produces more than half the roses sold in the United States.

Transportation and Communication

Getting around the huge state of Texas used to be quite a problem. Horse-drawn wagons and stagecoaches bounced over dirt roads— or no roads—with their wheels sinking into mudholes or breaking into splinters. By 1900, railroads connected hundreds of cities, and dirt roads reached even more. Today, Texas has more miles of roads and railroads than any other state.

Thirteen deepwater ports operate along Texas's Gulf Coast. Houston's port is the busiest. Judging by the tonnage it handles, it's the second-largest port in the country. The Gulf Intracoastal Waterway runs close to the coast all the way from Brownsville to New Orleans, Louisiana. From there, ships can head up the Mississippi River.

Air travel started early in Texas. The U.S. Army opened a flying school at Fort Sam Houston near San Antonio in 1910, and more than forty Texas military bases trained pilots during World

Houston is the state's busiest port.

War II. Today, the largest and busiest airports are the Dallas–Fort Worth International Airport and Houston Intercontinental Airport.

Communication

Tune in to a nightly news show, and you're bound to see a Texan. Some of the top newscasters in the country came from Texas—Sam Donaldson, Dan Rather, Stone Phillips, and Bill Moyers (born in

Oklahoma but raised in Texas). Television arrived in Texas in 1948, when Fort Worth's WBAP (today's KXAS) went on the air. Radio began with Dallas's WRR in 1920. Today, Texas has 125 TV stations, 95 cable systems, and more than 700 radio stations.

José Álvarez de Toledo published Texas's first newspaper, *Gaceta de Texas,* in 1813. Today, Texas publishes about 650 newspapers. The *Dallas Morning News*, founded in 1885, is respected nationwide. Its reporters have received many Pulitzer Prizes for journalism. Other major daily papers are the *Houston Chronicle,* the *Austin American-Statesman,* and the *Fort Worth Star-Telegram.*

The *Galveston News* first published the *Texas Almanac* in 1857. From this little ten-cent booklet, Texas families learned facts about their state's economy, population, history, and much more. Now published by the *Dallas Morning News,* the almanac has grown to almost 700 pages. Its articles, statistics, and maps cover Texas history, population, government, counties, environment, and arts.

Texas Monthly magazine is one of the best state magazines in the country. *Texas Highways* magazine is a popular travel and recreation guide published by the Texas Department of Transportation.

CHAPTER NINE

Who Are Texans?

Texas is so big that there's plenty of room for every-one. If all the people in Texas were spread out evenly across the state, there would be 64 people on every square mile (25 per sq km). If that's hard to imagine, try this. It's the same as if every man, woman, and child in the state had eight foot-ball fields for a living space!

Having fun at Fiesta Texas Theme Park

In reality, people prefer to live near cities where they can find good jobs, stores, schools, and entertainment. Four out of every five Texans live in cities and towns, while only one-fifth live in rural areas. The eastern half of the state is the most crowded. The most tightly packed areas are Dallas–Fort Worth, Houston, and San Antonio. Houston is the state's largest city. Next in order of size are Dallas, San Antonio, El Paso, Austin, and Fort Worth.

The 1990 census counted more than 17 million people in Texas. That made Texas third in the nation in number of residents, after California and New York. But 1994 estimates showed that Texas had pulled ahead of New York to become the country's second-largest state. Estimates in 1997 told the same story, showing Texas as number two with 19,439,000 people. That means that about one of every fourteen people in the whole nation lives in Texas.

Texas has been growing fast for decades. Since 1950, its population has more than doubled. The state grew 20 percent in the

Opposite: Many people—and their pets—enjoy living in Texas.

Latinos have a strong presence in Texas.

Young Chinese girls in costume at Corpus Christi

1980s, 27 percent in the 1970s, 17 percent in the 1960s, 24 percent in the 1950s, and 20 percent in the 1940s. More than 27 million people are expected to live in Texas by the year 2025.

Latino Texans

With Mexico just across the Rio Grande, it's not surprising that about 23 percent of the people in Texas claim a Mexican heritage. Some families along the border have lived in the area since Texas belonged to Mexico. Signs of Mexican culture are everywhere in Texas, but especially in the south. Mexican food and music spice up the air, and festivals and religious feasts are joyous and colorful celebrations.

The term "Latino" refers not only to people of Mexican ancestry, but also to people from any Spanish- or Portuguese-speaking culture. Some Latino Texans came from Central and South American countries, as well as Puerto Rico and Cuba. After Mexico, the most common places of origin for Latinos are El Salvador, Colombia, Guatemala, and Nicaragua. Altogether, Latinos make up about 26 percent of the state's population. Only California has a higher percentage of Latino residents.

Europeans and Asians

Only about one-tenth of the people who live in Texas were born outside the United States. But the ancestors of today's Texans came from all over the globe.

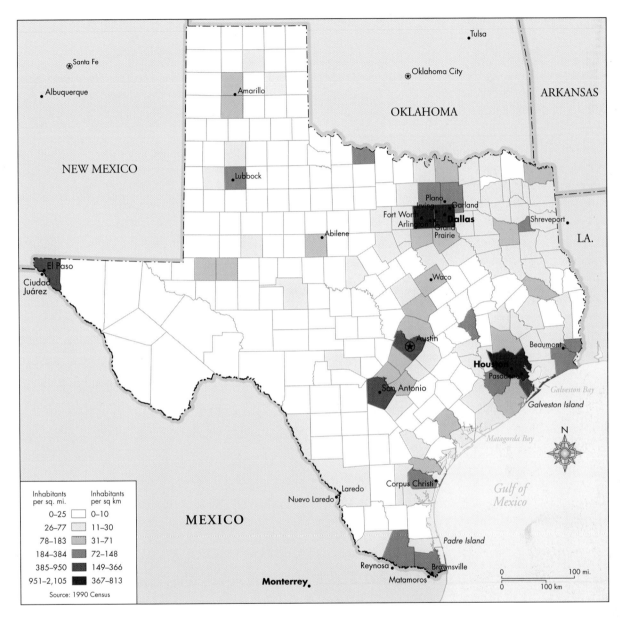

Inhabitants per sq. mi.	Inhabitants per sq km	
0–25	0–10	
26–77	11–30	
78–183	31–71	
184–384	72–148	
385–950	149–366	
951–2,105	367–813	

Source: 1990 Census

Many Texans are descendants of Irish, English, and Scottish settlers of the 1800s. Others are descended from German and Czech immigrants who settled in central and south Texas. Immigrants from Belgium and the Alsace region settled in Castroville, near San Antonio.

Texas's population density

In the late 1800s, Galveston was the nation's second-largest port of entry for immigrants, after New York City. Newcomers arrived from Germany, Poland, Norway, Sweden, France, and other European countries. Among them were Jewish people fleeing persecution in Eastern Europe. The immigrants fanned out across the state, bringing their traditional food, music, religion, and festivals to their new homes.

In east Texas, Cajun and Creole language, food, and culture spill over the border from Louisiana. They are remnants of French culture, dating from the time when Louisiana was a French colony.

Railroad companies in Texas imported Chinese workers to help build the railroads. Many of the workers stayed and opened restaurants, laundries, and other small businesses. Today, Texas's largest Chinese-American community is found in Houston.

Japanese people settled around Houston, too. They found that they could grow good rice crops on the low, flat fields. After the United States's involvement in the Vietnam War ended in 1973, thousands of Vietnamese, Cambodian, and Thai refugees settled in Texas. The ancestors of other Texans lived in India, the Philippines, Korea, Lebanon, and Greece.

African-Americans and Native Americans

African-Americans make up 12 percent of the population of Texas. Some are descended from slaves freed after the Civil War. Freedom gave them the chance to work as cowboys, farmers, and shop owners. Over the years, many more African-Americans came to work in the oil, aerospace, and chemical industries.

About 64,000 Native Americans live in Texas, and many more residents claim some Indian ancestry. The Tigua are the oldest ethnic group identified in the United States. They have lived in the area around Ysleta del Sur Reservation since 1682. The Tigua are Pueblo Indians who broke off from the Tiwa of New Mexico during the Pueblo Revolt of 1681.

More than a dozen Indian groups once lived in Texas, but the state has only three official Indian reservations today. One is the Alabama-Coushatta Indian Reservation in east Texas. These two tribes migrated from Alabama in the 1700s. The Texas Band Kickapoo Traditional Council lives on another reservation.

Students of different cultures attend school together.

A chili cook-off

How to Eat Like a Texan

Chili is serious business in Texas. Invented in San Antonio in the 1800s, it's now the state dish. Classic Texas chili is called Texas Red. As any chili fanatic will tell you, Texas Red has no beans, tomatoes, or bell peppers. But jalapeños or some other hot chili peppers are a must. Texas's chili cook-offs draw chili artists from all over the country.

Texas has more than 2,100 barbecue joints. Most serve barbecued beef brisket or beef ribs, but they might offer pork ribs or sausage, too. Proper barbecuing is a fine art. True professionals barbecue the meat over a pit lined with stones or raw steel. The fuel must be wood—post oak, mesquite, pecan, or hickory. Experts say the secret is to let the smoke—not the flame—cook the meat, and

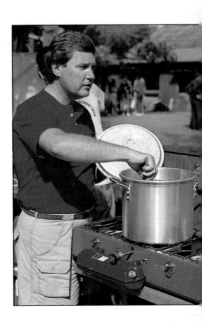

never put sauce on the meat before cooking—only afterward. However, some hard-core barbecuers insist that sauce is just a cover for bad meat.

If you're going to a fish fry in Texas, you're going to have catfish. Blue catfish is the favorite kind, served whole or cut into fillets, coated with cornmeal batter, and then deep-fried in an iron pot.

Chicken-fried steak is another Texas delicacy. It's made with round steak that's been pounded till it's tender. The almost-flat steak is coated with a batter of eggs, beer, and flour, then deep-fried till it's a crispy golden brown. The proper gravy for chicken-fried steak is made by taking the leftover frying fat and cooking it with flour and milk.

A "cowboy breakfast" consists of scrambled eggs, sausage, and sourdough biscuits slathered with brown gravy. Armadillo eggs are a delicious pork sausage and cheese appetizer. Cactus jelly is made from the fruit of the prickly pear cactus. Pralines are sugary candy with pecans mixed in. And some people swear that Texas's Blue Bell ice cream is the best in the country.

Mexican food is everywhere in Texas. Fajitas are thin strips of beef cooked with peppers and onions and wrapped in flour tortillas with guacamole and a tomato-and-spices mixture called pico de gallo. Picante or salsa are the hot sauces. Tacos, enchiladas, burritos, and tamales are most delicious in the southern towns. The ingredients and cooking methods are authentic—and the results are surprisingly different from what is served in Mexican fast-food restaurants.

Iced tea is the state's favorite thirst quencher. Rural diners often serve iced tea instead of water. Dr Pepper, invented in Waco,

Armadillo Eggs

These very popular appetizers are served in homes and restaurants all over Texas.

Ingredients:

- 2 eggs
- 1 6-oz. package of coating mix for pork, such as Shake-n-Bake
- 1 cup of grated cheddar cheese
- 1/2 pound of pork sausage, crumbled
- 1 1/2 cups of Bisquick mix
- 1 cup (8 ounces) of grated Monterey Jack cheese
- 1 26-oz. can of whole, seeded jalapeños

Directions:

Preheat the oven to 350°F.

Beat the eggs and put aside. Place the pork-coating mix in a small bowl and set aside.

Mix the cheddar cheese, sausage, and Bisquick together. Using a rolling pin, flatten the mixture until it's about 3/4 of an inch thick.

Stuff the Monterey Jack cheese into the jalapeño peppers. Wrap each pepper in the Bisquick mixture. Using your hands, roll each pepper into an egg shape (to make your armadillo eggs). Dip each armadillo egg into the beaten eggs, then roll in the pork-coating mix.

Arrange the armadillo eggs on a cookie sheet and bake for 20–25 minutes, or until crisp.

Makes 8 to 10 "eggs."

is another popular beverage. The Lone Star Beer brewery in Longview is the largest in the state. Texas wines have won national and international prizes. Some of the best vineyards grow around Lubbock.

Population of Texas's Major Cities (1990)

Houston	1,630,553
Dallas	1,006,877
San Antonio	935,933
El Paso	515,342
Austin	465,622
Fort Worth	447,619

Students at Texas A&M, the state's first public university

Three Centuries of Schools

The first schools in Texas were mission schools opened in the 1700s. A few public schools opened in the early 1800s, while Texas was still part of Mexico. However, they were not very useful to Anglo settlers because classes were taught only in Spanish. As early as 1832, Texans petitioned the Mexican government for English-language schools. When Texas won its independence, one-room wooden schoolhouses began to appear in cities and towns across the new republic.

In 1854, Texas set up a statewide English-language school system. Blacks and Mexicans, however, were generally excluded from Anglo schools. They attended separate schools, which began to receive state funds in the 1880s. In 1954, the U.S. Supreme Court ruled that "separate but equal" schools for different ethnic groups was unconstitutional. Since then, Texas's public schools have been open to all students.

Today, children in Texas begin school at age six. They must continue until they finish out the school year in which they turn sixteen years old. Texas has about 6,200 public elementary and secondary schools, with about 3.7 million students. The Texas Education Agency oversees all public schools in the state.

In some states, students are passed on to the next grade even if they don't quite deserve to pass. But in Texas, the state tries to make sure students really learn while they're in school. Students whose reading skills are still poor by third grade are not promoted. High school students who fail a class are barred for a time from taking part in extracurricular activities such as football or basketball. Also, high school seniors can graduate only if they pass basic reading, writing, and math tests.

University of Texas at Austin

Texas has about 180 colleges and universities. That's one of the highest counts in the nation. The University of Texas is the state's largest college system, with more than 100,000 students. Its main campus is in Austin, which enrolls about half the student body. Texas Agricultural and Mechanical University (Texas A&M), the state's first public college, emphasizes science and engineering. Other public universities are Texas Tech University in Lubbock and North Texas State University in Denton.

Private colleges include Houston's Rice University. Called the Harvard of the South, it's known for its high academic standards. Baylor University, a Baptist institution in Waco, was founded in 1845 under the Republic of Texas. Another church-supported school is Southern Methodist University (SMU) in Dallas.

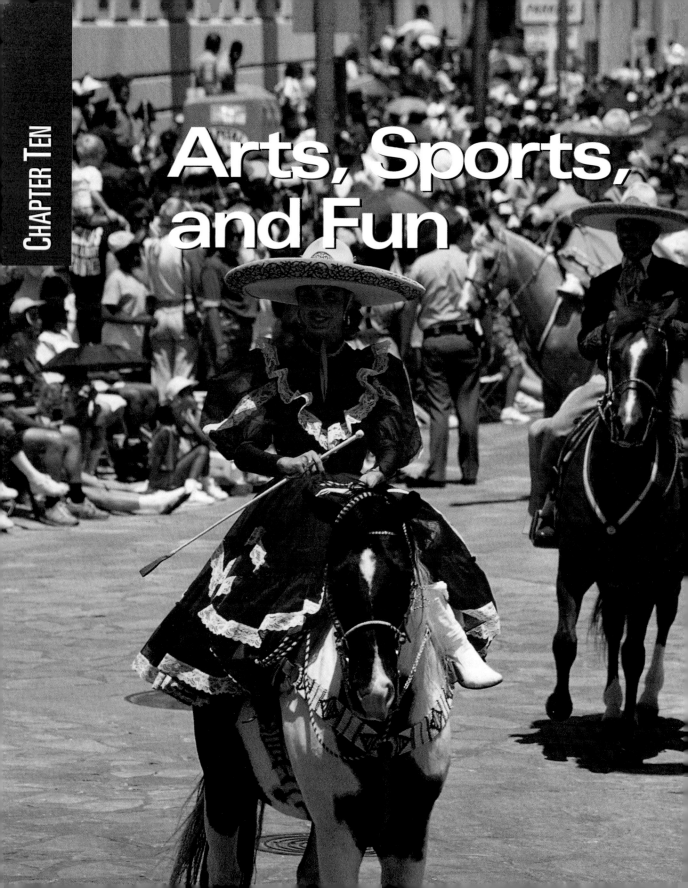

CHAPTER TEN

Arts, Sports, and Fun

The awards ceremony at the Van Cliburn International Piano Competition

Elvis Presley was the idol of millions of adoring fans in the late 1950s. But a new kind of star appeared on the music scene in 1958. A classical pianist from Fort Worth named Van Cliburn did what no one thought possible. He won the gold medal at the First International Tchaikovsky Piano Competition in Moscow, Russia, in the former Soviet Union.

The event made headlines around the world. No one expected that the prize would go to a Texan, playing Russian music on Russian soil. It was the height of the Cold War, after all, when the United States and the Soviet Union were sworn enemies. The prize committee even asked permission of Premier Nikita Khrushchev before awarding the prize to Cliburn.

Back in the United States, fans mobbed the tall, handsome Cliburn wherever he went. In one frenzied appearance, the door of his limousine was ripped off. An Elvis Presley fan club switched its loyalties and became a Van Cliburn fan club. Cliburn's recording of Tchaikovsky's first piano concerto was the first classical recording to sell more than a million copies. Dallas now hosts the Van Cliburn International Piano Competition every four years.

Roadhouses and Nightclubs

In the 1920s, Dallas music joints featured black blues artists Blind Lemon Jefferson, Huddie Ledbetter ("Leadbelly"), and

Opposite: The Battle of Flowers Parade in San Antonio

Van Cliburn

Harvey Lavan (Van) Cliburn Jr. (1934–) is a pianist known for his fine technique and romantic style. Born in Shreveport, Louisiana, he began studying piano at age three. The family soon moved to Kilgore, Texas, where Van gave his first public performance at age four. His mother was his piano teacher throughout his youth. After studying at the Juilliard School of Music in New York City, he made his first appearance with the New York Philharmonic in 1954. In 1958, Cliburn won the Tchaikovsky Piano Competition in Moscow, Russia. ■

T-Bone Walker. Houston's blues tradition revved up in the 1940s and early 1950s, with musicians such as Lightnin' Hopkins, Big Mama Thornton, and B. B. King.

Texas's blues styles had a great influence on early rock-and-rollers. Chuck Berry, Jerry Lee Lewis, and many others adopted the Texas blues artists' style. Later, Texas rockers Janis Joplin, Steve Miller, and ZZ Top were all inspired by their homegrown blues traditions.

From roadhouses to concert halls, the strains of country-western music fill the air. One of the nation's hottest country stars today is LeAnn Rimes of Garland. She recorded her first album, *Blue,* in 1996 when she was only fifteen years old. It immediately shot to the top of both the country and pop charts. Rimes went on to win many of country music's top honors.

Country-western stars Willie Nelson and Waylon Jennings, both Texas natives, helped make Austin a center for live music in the 1970s. But their style was different from the country music popular in Nashville, Tennessee. Rougher and more rock-oriented, it was called outlaw country music or redneck rock.

Jimmy Buffett, Lyle Lovett, Kris Kristofferson, Kenny Rogers, Jerry Jeff Walker, Stevie Ray Vaughan, and many others played in Austin's music clubs before they became famous. Today, with dozens of clubs and recording studios, Austin rivals Nashville as the music capital of the South. The music show *Austin City Limits* brings Austin's music scene to TV viewers throughout the country.

Every March, hundreds of bands play their hearts out in Austin nightclubs during the South by Southwest Music and Media

Scott Joplin

Scott Joplin (1868–1917) is known as the King of Ragtime Music. He was born near Linden and moved to Texarkana at around age seven. By then, he was already a good banjo player and was starting to play piano. As an adult, Joplin developed the ragtime style.

Joplin wrote his best-known piece, the "Maple Leaf Rag," while playing piano at the Maple Leaf Club in Sedalia, Missouri. Joplin's opera *Treemonisha* was the first opera written by an African-American. His music was featured in the 1973 movie *The Sting,* which won an Academy Award for its musical score. ▧

Conference. They're hoping to catch the attention of music critics and recording scouts.

Line dancing is popular around the country, and Texas is no exception. But many Texans swear that traditional one-on-one dancing is the only way to go. Country-western dancers show off their artistry in joints such as the Broken Spoke in Austin and in small-town roadhouses around the state.

Rock-and-roll legend Buddy Holly, a native of Lubbock, started out as a country-western singer. He died in a tragic plane crash in 1959, leaving behind "Peggy Sue" and many other hits. Lubbock erected a bronze monument in his honor.

Tejano music is popular in South Texas, especially along the Texas-Mexico border. *Tejano* is Spanish for "Texan." The music style is also called *conjunto* or Tex-Mex. A typical tejano band features an accordion, a 12-string guitar, and a violin. Accordions caught on in border towns in the late 1800s, when German immigrants brought their instruments to Texas. Modern tejano bands often include saxophone and keyboards, too. Fans are still grieving over the death of tejano singer Selena, who was killed in 1995.

Rocker Buddy Holly was a native of Lubbock.

The Dallas Symphony Orchestra is well known throughout the United States.

Classical Performing Arts

Most major cities in Texas have their own symphony orchestras and dance companies. Many cities have opera companies as well. The Dallas Symphony Orchestra, one of the best in the country, plays in the Morton H. Myerson Symphony Center, designed by architect I. M. Pei.

Houston's orchestra performs in the Jesse H. Jones Center for the Performing Arts, a complex of several theaters and concert halls. The Houston Grand Opera, appearing in the Wortham Theater Center, is the best known in the state.

Dance companies showcase both classical ballet and modern dance. Dancer and choreographer Alvin Ailey was born in Rogers, Texas. He moved to New York City, where his Alvin Ailey American Dance Theater became world famous.

Literature

Short-story writer O. Henry (William Sidney Porter) lived and worked in Austin for years. "The Ransom of Red Chief," "The Gift of the Magi," and many of his other stories still appear in TV versions today. Katherine Anne Porter, from Indian Creek, wrote short stories, novellas, and the novel *Ship of Fools*. Her *Collected Stories* won the 1966 Pulitzer Prize for fiction.

From Coronado's time till today, fortune hunters search through Texas's hills and dusty plains following rumors of buried treasure. This never-ending quest for gold is the subject of J. Frank Dobie's book *Coronado's Children*. Dobie has collected and published thirty volumes of Texas folklore and history. One of his most popular works is *A Vaquero of the Brush Country*. Fred Gipson was another Texas writer who brought local scenes to life. His 1956 novel *Old Yeller*, about a dog that got rabies, was made into a movie.

Another Texas dog has become a favorite of children (and adults) all over the world. It's Hank the Cowdog—hero, philosopher, and head of ranch security. When author John Erickson was a cowboy in the Panhandle, he worked with the real Hank. That's where he got the idea for his *Hank the Cowdog* stories. Erickson's advice to young writers is, "Write about something you know. Try to leave your readers better off than they were before." Erickson also tells tales of cowboy life in his many books for adults.

Taking a New Look

Typical Western movies and novels show a mythical Texas—a land of cattle drives, gunfights, honky-tonk saloons, and rugged heroes like John Wayne. But in modern times, this image doesn't really ring true. People in big cities and in eastern Texas have little contact with the Wild West scene. Also, the Texas myth tends to give a one-sided view of women, Mexican Americans, and other groups. Many Texas writers today are trying to show the state's history and culture in a more realistic way.

Among them are authors who explore their Mexican-American heritage in their writings. Pat Mora writes bilingual poems and sto-

O. Henry

William Sidney Porter (1862–1910) was a short-story writer who used the name O. Henry. Born in North Carolina, he moved to Texas at age twenty. There he worked as a ranch hand, draftsman, and bank teller. Porter started the *Rolling Stone*, an Austin weekly newspaper, and wrote a column for the *Houston Daily Post*. Charged with stealing from the bank, he was convicted and sent to an Ohio jail. He began writing short stories in prison and continued to write hundreds more after his release. His popular stories, many of them set in Texas, often end with a surprising twist. ■

ries for children. Sandra Cisneros tells of the joys and sorrows of Latina women and girls. Others are poet Ricardo Sánchez, short-story writer Alicia Gaspar de Alba, and novelists Roberta Fernández, Aristeo Brito, Arturo Islas, Tomás Rivera, and Montserrat Fontes.

Modern author Larry McMurtry, born in Wichita Falls, drew on his early life in Texas for his novels. They include *The Last Picture Show, Terms of Endearment,* and *Lonesome Dove,* which won a Pulitzer Prize in 1986. Robert Olen Butler won the 1993 Pulitzer Prize for his collection of Texas stories, *A Good Scent from a Strange Mountain.* Reginald McKnight's *The Kind of Light that Shines on Texas* received the O. Henry Award.

Art

Thanks to millions of dollars' worth of donations from wealthy Texans, the state has some of the finest art museums in the country. The Amon Carter Museum of Western Art in Fort Worth features paintings and bronze sculptures on Western themes. Fort Worth's Kimbell Art Museum holds a collection of portraits from the 1700s, as well as prehistoric and modern art. The Dallas Museum of Art displays art objects from Africa, Asia, Europe, and the Americas, dating from ancient to modern times. Other fine art museums are the Witte Museum in San Antonio and the Museum of Fine Arts in Houston.

German-born sculptor Elisabet Ney arrived in Texas in the 1870s. The state government asked her to make statues of Sam Houston and Stephen Austin. She moved from her ranch in Hempstead to Austin and began working in her studio-home, now a museum.

Ney's marble statues of the two Texas heroes now adorn the state capitol in Austin and Statuary Hall in Washington, D.C. Officials in Washington complained that Houston's statue was too tall, and Austin's was too short. Ney replied, "God Almighty made men; I only made the statues."

Georgia O'Keeffe painted enormous flowers, sheashells, and sun-bleached steers' skulls. She loved the West. From 1912 to 1918, she lived and taught art in the Texas Panhandle. Many of Texas's art museums exhibit her paintings.

Modern artist Robert Rauschenberg was born in Port Arthur. He settled in New York City, where he was one of the first pop art painters. Some of his work is a mixture of sculpture and painting. In the 1950s, he began adding motors and sound to his artworks.

Artist Georgia O'Keeffe lived and taught in Texas.

Dallas Cowboys quarterback Troy Aikman

Team Sports

Football fever is a statewide epidemic in the fall and winter. Professional, college, and high school football draws millions of fans. The entire state takes sides in the long-standing rivalry between the University of Texas Longhorns and the Texas A&M Aggies. Every New Year's Day, Dallas hosts the Cotton Bowl game, which pits regional college football champions against one another.

The Dallas Cowboys are Texas's only professional football team. Coach Tom Landry led the Cowboys to two Super Bowl championships in the 1970s. After several mediocre seasons, the Cowboys bounced back in the 1990s, winning the Super Bowl in 1993, 1994, and 1996. On the field, quarterback Troy Aikman and running back Emmit Smith were the picture of professional All-Pro athletes. In 1997, after several decades in Houston, the Houston Oilers moved to Nashville, Tennessee.

The Houston Astrodome

The Astrodome, opened in 1965, was the nation's first air-conditioned domed sports stadium. It was also the first stadium to use artificial turf. (Real grass can't grow there because the dome lacks direct sunlight, rain, and outdoor air.) The field surface called Astroturf was specially developed just for the Astrodome. Rising higher than an eighteen-story building, the stadium can seat up to 74,000 people. It's home to the Houston Astros baseball team. ■

Texas Aces

Texas is the breeding ground for some of baseball's finest pitchers. Perhaps the greatest pitcher of all time, Nolan Ryan, was born in Refugio. After winning the 1969 World Series with the New York Mets at age 22, Ryan became a superstar with the California Angels in the 1970s. His blinding fastball earned him the nickname "Ryan's Express." Ryan returned home in 1980 to play for the Houston Astros, and then with the Texas Rangers. He is a leader in almost every pitching category, but his 5,714 strikeouts are a record that may never be broken.

Born in Ohio, Roger Clemens spent his teenage years in Houston and began drawing attention as the ace of the University of Texas team that won the College World Series in 1983. As soon as he joined the Boston Red Sox, Clemens was a fearsome force. "Rocket Roger" struck out 20 Seattle Mariners on April 29, 1986, to set the major-league single-game record—and then ten years later he duplicated the feat against the Detroit Tigers. Clemens moved to the Toronto Blue Jays in 1997 and kept mowing down batters, notching his 3,000th career strikeout in 1998. He's just the eleventh pitcher ever to reach that mark. Clemens and his family still live in Houston.

In 1995, the Chicago Cubs drafted a 17-year-old Grand Prairie, Texas, pitcher who already had a 95-mile-an-hour fastball and had mastered the curveball. Three years later, Kerry Wood broke into the majors as a Cub and set the National League on fire. In just his fifth career game, Wood matched Clemens's 20-strikeout record in a one-hit shutout of the Houston Astros. While Texas baseball fans live and die by their Rangers and Astros, they also keep an eye to the north, watching their favorite fastball marvels. ■

Texas got its first professional baseball team in 1962 with the National League Houston Colt .45s. The team became the Astros three years later when it moved into the Astrodome. The Astros were joined by an American League neighbor in 1972, when the Washington Senators moved to Arlington, Texas, and were renamed the Texas Rangers.

Ride 'Em, Cowboy!

Not a week goes by without at least one rodeo going on somewhere in Texas. Many Texas colleges even offer rodeo courses. The most exciting—and dangerous—rodeo events are the "roughstock" events—bareback bronco riding, saddle bronco riding, and bull riding. The rider has to keep one hand free at all times and stay mounted for eight seconds. Other events are calf roping, steer wrestling (bulldogging), and barrel racing.

Texas holds hundreds of county fairs and livestock shows, too. The Texas State Fair is held in Dallas in late September to early October. This massive, three-week affair is the largest state fair in the country, with an attendance of more than 3 million visitors every year. It takes place in buildings erected for Texas's 1936 centennial celebration.

Celebrating Food

Food festivals tell a lot about Texans' taste—and pride. The Chilympiad—the "world's largest chili cook-off"—takes place in San Marcos every September. It's a hotly contested men's state championship, with chili, showmanship, and hot-sauce categories. Winners qualify to cook at Terlingua. About 5,000 "chiliheads" show up for Terlingua's International Championship Chili Cook-Off in November. It was started to prove that Texas-style chili is the world's best.

Texas hosts more than 200 barbecue competitions—more than the rest of the United States combined. Barbecue teams from all over the country compete in the National Championship Barbecue Cook-Off in Meridian.

"Babe" Didrikson Zaharias

Mildred Ella "Babe" Didrikson Zaharias (1911–1956), born in Port Arthur, was one of the greatest athletes of all time. In the 1932 Olympic Games, she won two medals in track-and-field events. Next she turned to golf and won the U.S. Women's Open golf championship three times (1948, 1950, 1954). Zaharias was also an excellent swimmer, tennis player, and rifle shooter. Her memorial museum is in Beaumont. ■

The Texas State Fair

Favorite crops have their day at the Strawberry Festival in Poteet, the Cantaloupe Festival in Pecos, and the Black-Eyed Pea Jamboree in Athens. Seafood lovers slurp up slithering delicacies at the Oysterfest in Fulton.

Luling holds its annual Watermelon Thump in June. Local beauties compete to be the year's Watermelon Thump Queen. But the highlight of the four-day festival is the world-champion watermelon-seed-spitting contest. Spitters vie to break the world record, set by Luling's last champ. That spitting distance—just short of 69 feet (21 m)—reigns in *The Guinness Book of World Records*.

Festivals for Every Culture

Latino festivals are familiar sights in Texas, especially in the south. Two of the biggest events are San Antonio's ten-day Fiesta in April and the state's many Cinco de Mayo (May 5) festivals. They're joyous and colorful celebrations of Mexican music, dancing, arts, and food. Diez y Seis, on September 16, is Mexican Independence Day. November 2 is *Día de los Muertos* (Day of the Dead), the Catholic feast of All Souls' Day. The celebration often begins on October 31, with processions, costumes, and skull- or skeleton-shaped candies, masks, and puppets. It's not a morbid festival, but a joyful time for remembering loved ones.

In February, people from both sides of the border join in to celebrate Brownsville's Charro Days and Laredo's Washington's Birthday festival. *Charreadas* (Mexican rodeos) are the highlight of Charro Days, while Laredo's festivities include a jalapeño-eating contest.

Cajun and Creole communities in southeast Texas celebrate Mardi Gras, just as their neighbors in Louisiana do. The revelry ends before Ash Wednesday ushers in the pre-Easter Lenten season. Galveston's Mardi Gras is the grandest, with ten days of parades, floats, parties, and Cajun and Creole food.

Ennis holds its National Polka Festival in May. It's part of a whole weekend of Czech feasting and polka dancing. October is the time for Oktoberfests in German communities such as Fredericksburg.

Juneteenth celebrates June 19, 1865—the day that slaves in Texas learned they had been freed by the Emancipation Proclamation of 1863. Festivities take place throughout the state, while Houston puts on Juneteenth blues and gospel festivals. Although Juneteenth started in Galveston, the celebration has spread to many other states around the country. In Texas, it's a state holiday.

"An international party with a Texas twist"—that's what the Institute of Texan Cultures calls its Texas Folklife Festival. The party in San Antonio lasts for four days in August. Texans from more than forty different cultures serve food, demonstrate crafts, sing, dance, and tell traditional tales.

With a barbecued rib in one hand and a Polish pierogi (dumpling) in the other, watching African folk dancers as a tejano band wails in the distance, a visitor can't help feeling that Texas is the center of the world.

Timeline

United States History

The first permanent British settlement is established in North America at Jamestown. **1607**

Pilgrims found Plymouth Colony, the second permanent British settlement. **1620**

America declares its independence from England. **1776**

The Treaty of Paris officially ends the Revolutionary War in America. **1783**

The U.S. Constitution is written. **1787**

The Louisiana Purchase almost Doubles the size of the United States. **1803**

The United States and Britain fight the War of 1812. **1812–15**

Texas State History

1519 Alonso Álvarez de Piñeda sails into the Rio Grande and maps the coast of Texas

1528 Cabeza da Vaca writes about Texas after being captured by Karankawa Indians, escaping, and fleeing to what is now California

1682 Texas's first mission is built at Ysleta

1718 Mission San Antonio de Valero is built, later becoming the city of San Antonio

1821 Texas becomes a state within the republic of Mexico

1822 Colonists establish the first settlement, Austin's Colony, under the leadership of Stephen Fuller Austin

1836 Texas soldiers claim San Antonio. Against thousands of Mexican soldiers, 189 Texan troops defend the Alamo. On April 21, Mexican general Santa Anna surrenders to Sam Houston at San Jacinto, giving Texas its independence.

1845 Texas ratifies its constitution and becomes the twenty-eighth state on December 29

United States History

The North and South fight **1861–65** ach other in the American Civil War.

The United States is **1917–18** involved in World War I.

The stock market crashes, **1929** plunging the United States into the Great Depression.

The United States **1941–45** fights in World War II.
The United States becomes a **1945** charter member of the U.N.

The United States **1951–53** fights in the Korean War.

The U.S. Congress enacts a series of **1964** groundbreaking civil rights laws.

The United States **1964–73** engages in the Vietnam War.

The United States and other **1991** nations fight the brief Persian Gulf War against Iraq.

Texas State History

1846 The Mexican-American War erupts over a land dispute

1861 Texas secedes from the Union

1865 The last battle of the Civil War is fought on Palmito Hill on May 12 and 13.

1870 Texas is readmitted to the Union

1901 The Spindletop oil well, the first in Texas, begins to gush crude oil

1958 Texas Instruments develops the first silicon chip

1963 President John F. Kennedy is assassinated in Dallas on November 22

1964 The Manned Spacecraft Center opens in Houston

Fast Facts

State capitol

Statehood date	December 29, 1845, the 28th state
Origin of state name	Variant of Caddo Indian word meaning "friends"
State capital	Austin
State nickname	Lone Star State
State motto	Friendship
State bird	Mockingbird
State flower	Bluebonnet
State gemstone	Topaz
State plant	Prickly pear cactus
State fish	Guadalupe bass
State insect	Monarch butterfly
State song	"Texas, Our Texas"
State tree	Pecan
State fair	Mid-October at Dallas
Total area; rank	267,277 sq. mi. (692,247 sq km); 2nd

San Antonio

Bluebonnet

Land; rank	261,914 sq. mi. (678,357 sq km); 2nd
Water; rank	5,363 sq. mi. (13,890 sq km); 8th
Inland water; **rank**	4,959 sq. mi. (12,844 sq km); 2nd
Coastal water; **rank**	404 sq. mi. (1,046 sq km); 14th
Geographic center	McCulloch, 15 miles (39 km) northeast of Brady
Latitude and longitude	Texas is located approximately between 93° 31' and 106° 38' W and 25° 50' and 36° 30' N
Highest point	Guadalupe Peak, 8,751 feet (2,667 m)
Lowest point	Sea level along the Gulf of Mexico
Largest city	Houston
Number of counties	254
Longest river	Rio Grande, 1,240 miles (1,996 km)
Population; rank	17,059,805 (1990 census); 3rd
Density	64 persons per sq. mi. (25 per sq km)
Population distribution	80% urban, 20% rural

Ethnic distribution (does not equal 100%)

White	78.21%
Hispanic	25.55%
African-American	11.90%
Other	10.62%
Asian and Pacific Islanders	1.88%
Native American	0.39%

Record high temperature	120°F (49°C) at Seymour on August 12, 1936
Record low temperature	−23°F (−31°C) at Julia on February 12, 1899 and at Seminole on February 8, 1933

Rio Grande

Texans

Average July
temperature 83°F (28°C)

Average January
temperature 46°F (8°C)

Average annual
precipitation 27 inches (67 cm)

Natural Areas and Historic Sites
National Parks
Big Bend sits on the Rio Grande right at the river's bend, on 801,163 acres (324,223 ha) in West Texas. Its landscapes range from desert to mountain.

Guadalupe Mountains include the highest peak in Texas, canyons, and parts of Earth's largest Permian limestone fossil reef.

National Monument
At *Alibates Flint Quarries National Monument*, visitors can see the pits in the flint rock made by ancient settlers.

National Recreation Areas
Amistad, on the Mexico-U.S. border, boasts huge limestone cliffs. Tourists can also see rock art, ancient fibers, and parts of tools left by 300 generations of hunters and gatherers.

Lake Meredith was formed by Sanford Dam in the Texas Panhandle's High Plains. More than a million visitors per year come to see the vistas and plantlife of the arid plains.

National Preserve
Big Thicket was formed to protect the region where the prairies of the west, hardwood forests of the east, wetlands of the south, and desert-lands of the southwest come together.

National Memorial
Chamizal National Memorial honors the 1963 treaty between the United States and Mexico, which ended a 100-year border dispute.

Guadalupe Mountains

Palo Duro Canyon

National Historical Parks

Lyndon B. Johnson honors the thirty-sixth president of the United States. Visitors can follow Johnson's ancestry and boyhood, learn about his achievements, and see his gravesite.

San Antonio Missions is the site of four missions—San Juan, Concepción, San José, and Espada—built during the Spanish colonization of Mexico and the Southwest.

National Historic Sites

Fort Davis was an important military site in the late 1800s, when soldiers guarded travelers on the San Antonio–El Paso Road. It is considered a well-preserved fort in the Southwest.

Palo Alto Battlefield honors the site of the first confrontation between Mexican and U.S. troops during the Mexican-American War.

National Wild and Scenic River

Rio Grande is the most undeveloped portion of the river that borders the United States and Mexico. The 196-mile (315-km) length is overseen by Big Bend National Park.

National Seashore

Padre Island is the longest barrier island on Earth that hasn't been developed. Tourists can enjoy various types of water activities, from surfing to sailing.

Sports Teams

NCAA Teams (Division 1)

Baylor University Bears

Lamar University Cardinals

Prairie View A&M University Panthers

Rice University Owls

Sam Houston State University Bearkats

Southern Methodist University Mustangs

Southwest Texas State University Bobcats

At Mission San José

Troy Aikman

Stephen F. Austin State University Lumberjacks

Texas A&M University Aggies

Texas Christian University Horned Frogs

Texas Southern University Tigers

Texas Tech University Red Raiders

University of Houston Cougars

University of North Texas Eagles

University of Texas–Austin Longhorns

University of Texas–Pan American Broncos

University of Texas–San Antonio Roadrunners

Major League Baseball
Houston Astros

Texas Rangers

National Basketball Association
San Antonio Spurs

Dallas Mavericks

Houston Rockets

National Football League
Dallas Cowboys

National Hockey League
Dallas Stars

Houston Aeros

Women's National Basketball Association
Houston Comets

Cultural Institutions
Libraries
The *Mary Evelyn Blagg-Huey Library* in Denton, part of the Texas Women's University Libraries system, contains an extensive collec-

Dallas Museum of Art

tion of material about women—one of only three large collections in the United States.

The Daughters of the Republic of Texas Library in San Antonio is part of the Alamo, containing materials about the site and Texas history.

Texas State Library and Archives Commission in Austin contains historical records about the state along with geneaological collections and the state archives.

Museums

The *Kimbell Art Museum* in Fort Worth is world renowned for its art exhibitions and stunning collections.

The *McAllen International Museum* holds one of the country's largest collections of Latin American folk art and puts on several science and art exhibitions each year.

The *Panhandle-Plains Historical Museum* in Canyon keeps the history of northwest Texas alive. Built in 1933, it is the biggest and oldest heritage museum in Texas.

Performing Arts

Texas has four opera companies, six symphony orchestras, five dance companies, and two professional theater companies.

Universities and Colleges

In the mid-1990s, Texas had 106 public and 72 private institutions of higher learning.

University of Texas at Austin

Annual Events

January–March

Southwestern Exposition and Fat Stock Show and Rodeo in Fort Worth (January or February)

Texas Citrus Festival in Mission (January or February)

Charro Days Festival in Brownsville (February)

San Antonio Stock Show and Rodeo (February)

George Washington's Birthday festival in Laredo (February)

Houston Livestock Show and Rodeo Exposition (February–March)

Dallas Video Festival (March)

Oysterfest in Fulton (March)

Texas Independence Day (March 2)

April–June

Mardi Gras in Galveston and other cities (spring)

Annual Poteet Strawberry Festival (April)

Fiesta San Antonio in San Antonio (April)

Jefferson Historical Pilgrimage in Jefferson (April or May)

Buccaneer Days in Corpus Christi (April or May)

National Polka Festival in Ennis (May)

Cinco de Mayo celebration in Austin and other cities (May 5)

Kerrville Folk Festival (late May and early June)

Cantaloupe Festival in Pecos (June)

Juneteenth festivals in Galveston and other cities (June 19)

Scottish Festival and Highland Games in Arlington (June)

Watermelon Thump in Luling (June)

July–September

Shakespeare Festival in Odessa (summer)

Black-Eyed Pea Jamboree in Athens (July)

Texas Cowboy Reunion and Rodeo in Stamford (July)

National Championship Barbecue Cook-Off in Meridian (August)

Texas Folklife Festival in San Antonio (August)

Diez y Seis, or Mexican Independence Day, in various cities
   (September 16)

Rice Festival in Winnie (September or October)

State Fair in Dallas (late September and early October)

October–December

East Texas Yamboree in Gilmer (October)

Oktoberfest in Fredericksburg and other cities (October)

Texas Rose Festival in Tyler (October)

Confederate Airshow in Midland (October)

International Championship Chili Cook-Off in Terlingua (November)

Wurstfest in New Braunfels (November)

Día de los Muertos (Day of the Dead) in various cities (October 31–November 2)

Festival of the Lights in San Antonio (December)

Famous People

Joan Crawford (1908–1977)	Actress
Dwight David Eisenhower (1890–1969)	Military leader and U.S. president
James Edward Ferguson (1871–1944)	Public official
Miriam A. Ferguson (1875–1961)	Public official
John Nance Garner (1868–1967)	U.S. vice president
Howard Robard Hughes (1905–1976)	Industrialist, aviator, motion-picture producer
Lyndon Baines Johnson (1908–1973)	U.S. president
Audie Murphy (1924–1971)	Soldier and actor
Sandra Day O'Connor (1930–)	Supreme Court justice
Katherine Anne Porter (1890–1980)	Author
Wiley Post (1899–1935)	Aviator
Mildred Ella (Babe) Didrikson Zaharias (1911–1956)	Athlete

To Find Out More

History

- Bredeson, Carmen. *Texas*. New York: Marshall Cavendish, 1997.

- Burnett, Carolyn Mitchell. Illustrated by Jo Kay Wilson. *The First Texans*. Austin, Tex.: Eakin Publications, 1995.

- Fradin, Dennis Brindell. *Texas*. Chicago: Childrens Press, 1992.

- Green, Carl R., and William R. Sanford. *Judge Roy Bean*. Outlaws and Lawmen of the Wild West series. Springfield, N.J.: Enslow Publishers, Inc., 1995.

- Johnson, Drew D., and Cynthia Brantley Johnson. *Kidding Around Austin : What to Do, Where to Go, and How to Have Fun in Austin*. Santa Fe, N.M.: John Muir Publications, 1997.

- McComb, David G. *Texas: An Illustrated History*. New York: Oxford University Press, 1995.

- Pelta, Kathy. *Texas*. Minneapolis: Lerner Publications, 1994.

- Sorrels, Roy. *The Alamo in American History*. Springfield, N.J.: Enslow Publishers, Inc., 1996.

- Thompson, Kathleen. *Texas*. Austin, Tex.: Raintree/Steck Vaughn, 1996.

- Wills, Charles A. *A Historical Album of Texas*. Brookfield, Conn.: Millbrook, 1995.

Fiction

- Gipson, Fred. *Old Yeller*. New York: HarperTrophy, 1990.

Paulsen, Gary. *Sisters/Hermanas*. Translated by Gloria De Aragon Andujar. San Diego: Gulliver Books, 1994.

Biographies

Burandt, Harriet. *Tales from the Homeplace: Adventures of a Texas Farm Girl*. New York: Henry Holt & Company, 1997.

Bustard, Anne. *T Is for Texas*. Stillwater, Minn.: Voyageur Press, 1989.

Cardona, Rodolfo. *Henry Cisneros*. Broomall, Penn.: Chelsea House, 1994.

Lightfoot, D. J. *Trail Fever: The Life of a Texas Cowboy*. New York: Lothrop Lee & Shepard, 1992.

Martinez, Elizabeth. *Henry Cisneros : Mexican American Leader*. Brookfield, Conn.: Millbrook, 1993.

Preston, Katherine. *Scott Joplin*. Broomall, Penn.: Chelsea House, 1989.

Sanford, William R., and Carl R. Green. *Davy Crockett: Defender of the Alamo*. Springfield, N.J.: Enslow, 1996.

Websites

State of Texas Government
http://www.state.tx.us
Official website for the Texas state government

Texas State Electronic Library
http://link.tsl.state.tx.us/index.html
Connects users to information on Texas

Addresses

Texas Parks and Wildlife
4200 Smith School Road
Austin, TX 78744
For information on the state's many parks

Office of the Governor
P.O. Box 12428
Austin, TX 78711-2428
To contact Texas's highest elected official

Texas Historical Commission
History Divisions Program
P.O. Box 12276
Austin, TX 78711-2276
Preserves historical information and cultural landmarks in Texas

Index

Page numbers in *italics* indicate illustrations.

Meet the Author

Ann Heinrichs fell in love with faraway places while reading Doctor Dolittle books as a child. She has traveled through most of the United States and several countries in Europe, as well as northwest Africa, the Middle East, and east Asia.

Ann's earliest impressions of Texas came from her grandfather, who spent long, lazy summer afternoons telling tales of his childhood there—tales of walking miles to his one-room schoolhouse and back, rain or shine. Since then, both business and pleasure have taken her to Texas many times.

"Trips are fun, but the real work—tracking down all the factual information for a book—begins at the library. I head straight for the reference department. Some of my favorite resources are statistical abstracts and the library's computer databases.

"For this book, I also read local newspapers from several cities in Texas. The internet was a super research tool, too. The state library and various state agencies have websites that are chock full of information.

"To me, writing nonfiction is a bigger challenge than writing fiction. With nonfiction, you can't just dream something up—everything has to be researched. When I uncover the facts, they always turn out to be more spectacular than fiction could ever be."

Ann Heinrichs grew up in Fort Smith, Arkansas, and now lives in Chicago. She is the author of more than thirty books for children and young adults on American, Asian, and African history and culture. Several of her books have received state and national awards.

Heinrichs has also written numerous newspaper, magazine, and encyclopedia articles and critical reviews. As an advertising copywriter, she has covered everything from plumbing hardware to Oriental rugs and porcelain dolls. She holds a bachelor's and master's degree in piano performance. These days, her performing arts are t'ai chi chuan and kung fu sword.

Photo Credits